Freedom of Religion and Its Regulation in Nigeria

Law and Religion

Volumes published in this Brill Research Perspectives title are listed at *brill.com/rplr*

Freedom of Religion and Its Regulation in Nigeria

Analysis of Preaching Board Laws in Some States of Northern Nigeria

By

Ahmed Salisu Garba

BRILL

LEIDEN | BOSTON

This paperback book edition is simultaneously published as issue 1.4 (2017) of *Law and Region*, DOI 10.1163/24682993-12340004.

Library of Congress Control Number: 2018931175

Typeface for the Latin, Greek, and Cyrillic scripts: "Brill". See and download: brill.com/brill-typeface.

ISBN 978-90-04-35311-4 (paperback)
ISBN 978-90-04-35312-1 (e-book)

This book is printed on acid-free paper and produced in a sustainable manner.

Contents

Freedom of Religion and Its Regulation in Nigeria: Analysis of Preaching Board Laws in Some States of Northern Nigeria

Ahmed Salisu Garba

Abstract

The re-enactment of religious preaching board laws to regulate religious preaching in some states of Northern Nigeria generated debates between Government on the one hand and religious/human rights groups on the other. This research examines the Preaching Board Laws of Kano, Borno and Kaduna States in Northern Nigeria through the prism of the Nigerian Constitution and other democratic norms that relate to the right to freedom of religion in all democratic orders. It applies argumentative methodology to raise and analyse the following questions: how reasonable and justifiable are these religious preaching board laws in a democratic Nigeria?; what gave rise to the enactment of these laws in the states under study?; what judicial review mechanism would be employed to determine their reasonableness and justifiability in a democracy?; how do they accord with the freedom of religion clause in the Constitution of the Federal Republic of Nigeria? The research establishes that some of the provisions of these laws are inconsistent with the provisions of the Nigerian Constitution and, by extension, international freedom of religion norms operating in all democratic orders. Second, Nigerian courts have not developed suitable balancing mechanisms for resolving conflicts between the right of the state to regulate and citizens' right to freedom of religion otherwise called the two competing rights, in the light of which the research calls for the amendment of the laws to accord with the provisions of the Constitution and international freedom of religion norms acceptable in all democracies. The paper further recommends a harmonised proportionality test or judicial standard of review based on Nigeria's religion-state relations and local experience for the use of courts, legislators and administrative agents coming face to face with this type of conflict in their official capacity.

* Ahmed S. Garba, Lecturer, Department of Public Law, Faculty of Law, Bauchi State University, Gadau, Bauchi State, Nigeria.

 | DOI 10.1163/9789004353121_002

Keywords

religion – regulation – preaching boards – democratic society – freedom of religion

Introduction

The re-enactment of religious preaching board laws as a social control mechanism to regulate religious preaching in some states of Northern Nigeria has remained a subject of debate between Government on the one hand and religious/human rights groups on the other. The re-enactment process may have started in 2000 when some states expanded the scope of the application of Sharia Laws in Northern Nigeria. Borno, Kaduna, Niger and Katsina States started their own processes of the re-enactment of religious preaching laws in reaction to the crises associated with Muslim religious groups in their areas. Borno State amended its religious preaching board law in 2010[1] in response to the Boko Haram imbroglio in the state. The legislative action of Borno State prompted Katsina[2] and Niger[3] States to propose analogous bills in 2011 and 2014 respectively to amend their religious preaching board laws also in reaction to similar skirmishes associated with some Islamic religious groups in the two states.[4] In a similar manner, the government of Kaduna State proposed a bill, among other social control measures, for a law to regulate religious preaching in the state in reaction to the Army-Shi'ite uncomfortable situation which occurred on 12 December 2015 in the city of Zaria in Kaduna State.[5]

Apart from the sporadic legislative activity of some Northern States described above, there have also been calls and agitations from different quarters for the regulation of religious preaching. For example, different panels of

1 The Borno State Admonishing and Interpretation Edict of 1977 was repealed by the Borno State Islamic Religious Preaching Law 1981 in so far as it applied to Islamic religious preaching.

2 See the Katsina State Islamic Education and Preaching Law of 2011. This Law consolidated two laws that had been in operation since 1991 in the State. They are the Islamic Education Bureau Law of 1991 and the Religious Preaching Regulation of 1991.

3 See the Niger State Islamic Religious Preaching Edict of 1979 which was repealed and replaced in 1985. For Sokoto State see the Certain Religious Preaching Edict of 1979. This was amended in 1984; repealed and replaced in 1986.

4 Aisha Wakaso, *This Day Newspaper* (Tuesday, 1 July 2014) Page 12. Also see Katsina State Government's Publication, *New Nigeria News*, 22 September 2011.

5 A bill for a law to substitute the Kaduna State Regulation of Religious Preaching (Amendment) Edict No. 6 of 1996.

inquiry set up by the Federal Government of Nigeria to investigate the immediate and remote causes of some crises in Northern Nigeria have advocated for the regulation of religious preaching, among other measures, for the purpose of peace in Nigeria.[6] Also, in 2014, the former Chief Justice of Nigeria, the Honourable Justice Dahiru Mustapha, called for the regulation of public religious preaching to control religious preaching by those he called "incompetent Islamic scholars in order to solve the problem of insurgency" in Northern Nigeria.[7]

This research examines and analyses the religious preaching board laws of Borno, Kano[8] and Kaduna States, arguing that they are not reasonable in a democratic society like Nigeria and that the states, in employing them, are not achieving their overall aims regarding the conflicts they were responding to in their various domains. To succeed in their objectives, the states' responses must accord with the Nigerian Constitution and other democratic norms regarding freedom of religion in democratic societies around the world. The choice of these states from Sokoto,[9] Bauchi,[10] Plateau,[11] Katsina, Jigawa, Kebbi, Yobe, Zamfara, Gombe, Yobe and Nassarawa States which also have preaching board laws is because, with the exception of Kaduna State, Kano and Borno were the first two states to enact the first sets of religious preaching board laws in northern Nigeria: Kano in 1970 and Borno in 1977. Second, the so-called Maitatsine riots happened in these states and were responded to with the enactment of religious preaching laws. For example, the main Maitatsine uprising took place

6 See: The White Paper on the Report of the Presidential Committee on the Security Challenges in North-Eastern Zone of Nigeria, para. 112 at p. 23. See also The White Paper of the Federal Government Investigative Panel on the 2011 Election Violence and Civil Disturbances, para. 66(a)(b) and (c) at p. 17.

7 *'Insurgency, It's time to regulate public preaching'*, in *Daily Trust News Paper*, 21 May 2014, p. 5.

8 See the Kano Local Government Authority (Control of Quranic Interpretation and Admonishing) Rules 1970. This became the Kano Local Government Law No. 3, 1970. This law was repealed by the Kano State Religious Preaching Edict of 1985. It should be noted that in 1982 the Kano State House of Assembly enacted another law called the Kano State Council for Islamic Affairs Law 1982 which was also repealed by a law with the same title in 1985.

9 See the Niger State Islamic Religious Preaching Edict of 1979 which was repealed replaced in 1985). For Sokoto see The Certain Religious Preaching Edict of 1979. This was amended in 1984; repealed and replaced in 1986.

10 See the Bauchi State Religious Preaching Law of 1984. This Law was suspended by the Bauchi State Religious Preaching (suspension) Law of 1987.

11 See: the Plateau State Regulation of Public Preaching Edict of 1986.

in 1980 in Kano State. Its offshoot in 1982 however, happened in Borno and Kaduna States. Between 1967 and 1980 Kano State in particular had to contend with problems associated with religious groups called Gardawa, Izala and Maitatsine in response to which the state amended its religious preaching law. For their part, Borno and Kaduna States jointly experienced the spill-over of the Gardawa and Maitatsine riots which started in Kano between 26 and 29 October 1982 and in Borno and Rigassa between 26 and 30 October 1982 and which is popularly called the *Bullum Kuttu* uprising. In addition, Borno and Kano also experienced the recent Boko Haram uprising while Kaduna had to contend with the Shi'ites' confrontation with a military convoy of the Chief of the Army Staff in Decmber 2015. In all of these instances the states reacted, (among other responses) by effecting changes in their religious preaching legislation.

To establish this thesis, the research raises and analyses the following questions: first, what gave rise to the enactment of these laws in the states under study? second, how reasonable and justifiable are these religious preaching board laws in a democratic Nigeria? third, what judicial review mechanism would be employed to determine their reasonability and justifiability in a democracy? and fourth, how do they accord with the freedom of religion clause in the Constitution of the Federal Republic of Nigeria? The paper adopts the argumentative methodology in its analysis of the issues raised.

The consequence of not finding answers to these questions is that a vital constitutional issue will remain a conundrum, a fact which may make room for manipulation under the guise of the discretionary exercise of power by the prescribed authorities against minority religious groups. Such inherent abuse may lead to public loss of confidence in the judiciary and the government the consequence of which is avoidable breakdown of law and order in society. Corroboratively, research has shown that the process of exercising discretion by courts in some legal orders is prone to bias where minority religious groups in the society are involved.[12] In addition, courts tend to accept even inadmissible evidence against such minority religious groups when such evidence supports their prejudice against those groups.[13] Guidance is therefore needed for the judiciary to be able to discharge its function prudently.

To achieve its objectives, this research provides a detailed analysis of the religious preaching board laws of Kano, Borno, and Kaduna States. First, after reviewing some literature on the comparative regulation of religion in Nigeria

12 James T. Richardson (ed.), *Regulating Religion: Case Studies from Around the Globe*, (Kluwer Academic/Plenum Publishers, New York, 2004) pp. 1–15.

13 Ibid.

and the world at large, the work examines the history of the regulation of preaching in Nigeria and its effects on various religious groups in order to understand what gave rise to the enactment of the laws in the states under study. Second, the paper analyses the provisions of the religious preaching laws of the states under study and their likely effect on religious groups in the states, particularly religious minorities. Third, the paper recommends, among other things, that of the different assessment tests that exist today, the European Court of Human Rights' judicial review mechanism is the most suitable to the Nigerian environment in comparison with those of Germany, the United States of America and Canada. This is because it is more sensitive to people's environment than the others.

Conceptual Clarification

There is a need to clarify the meaning of some concepts as applied in this work: "religion", "preaching boards", "regulation of religious preaching" and "democratic society". Research indicates that defining religion for legal reasons is a difficult task.[14] In view of this difficulty and for the purpose of this research, therefore, religion means Islam or Christianity or both, as may be determined by the context. On the meaning of regulation, Black's Law Dictionary defines it as "the act or process of controlling by rule or restriction."[15] In a work of this nature, lexical meanings are of little assistance since they only provide clues without relating them to the subject matter or stating who did what and why. For example, on the present topic the lexical meaning will not indicate whether or not a particular restriction on the right to freedom of religion is imposed by the government or some other bodies in their private capacities. In this regard, the Grims and Finkes'[16] approach may be more relevant to this work, however with a little modification. They defined regulation in two ways. First, government regulation which means "the restrictions placed on the practice,

14 Robin C., *The Elusive Meaning of Religious Equality* 83 Wash. U. L. Q. 1529 2005, at p. 1540, available at http://heinonline.org (accessed on Friday, 4 October 2013), 13:41:37; Jeffrey L. O., '*Constitutional* "Religion" A *Survey of First Amendment Definitions of Religion*' 6 Tex. F. on C.L. & C.R. 117 2001–2002, at p. 122, available at http://heinonline.org (accessed on Friday, 4 October 2013) 13:34:07.

15 Bryan A. Garner, *Black's Law Dictionary, 9th edition* (U.S.A.: West-A Thomson Reuters Business, 2014), 1398.

16 Brian J. Grim and Roger Finke, *International Religion Index: Government Favoritism, and Social Regulation of Religion* (Interdisciplinary Journal of Research on Religion, 2006) Vol. 2, Article 1, p. 7.

profession, or selection of religion by the official laws, policies, or administrative actions of the state." They call this "*de jure*" regulation which means a situation where government imposes an unfair law or policy or both on a religion or a religious group based on a perceived danger or benefit of that religion or its practice in the public domain. Second social regulation which means "the restrictions placed on the practice, profession, or selection of religion by other religious groups, associations, or the culture at large." They call this "*de facto*" regulation. This is when it is based on the influence of a dominant religion or other associations or even the culture of the majority in a society the influence of which may indirectly persuade authorities to enact and enforce laws or policies or both that were unjust or discriminatory to other minority religious groups for the benefit of that dominant religion.

With due respect to the learned authors, this classification is ambiguous and misleading. First, their approach negates the possibility of having a combination of the two groups to produce a third one based on the link of the role of the religion-state relationship in the regulation of freedom of religion. Government regulation in its pure form is realistic only in a secular regime while social regulation is likely under a non-secular regime. This is because in a purely secular regime there is separation of religion and the state which indicates that religion may not influence anything as in France, China and the former Soviet Union. In a non-secular regime however, dominant religious groups' ideologies do influence state regulation of freedom of religion and other government policies. In summary, the argument here is that a purely secular regime can regulate without the influence of any external dominant religious ideology except the state's dominant secular ideology which the government wants to protect. So also, where the regime is one that shows favouritism to one or two religions as in the case of Nigeria and other theorcratic states, the favoured religion or religions do influence the regulation of freedom of religion in a way that burdens minority religious groups in the state. An example of this scenario is the nature of the regulation of religious preaching in Northern Nigeria and theocratic countries like Iran and Saudi Arabia.

In view of the above therefore, where it is shown that a particular regulatory regime is influenced by a dominant religious ideology in society, then a proper classification would be to call it collaborative, cooperative, joint or supportive regulation which may not be purely government regulation or purely social regulation but a combination of both. This is notwithstanding whether the influence is direct or indirect. But we may have restrictions placed on the freedom of religion by society through intimidation and societal pressure or even cultural practices. This is more akin to unlawful restriction than social regulation. Following the above explanation, it can be stated that the religion-state relationship plays an important role in the regulation of freedom of religion, and understanding this role will help clarify the difference between government regulation and social regulation.

Second, the approach equalises two unequal subjects. In a democracy the government can legitimately regulate the right to freedom of religion while bodies such as religious cartels or dominant religious groups cannot. Instead, they apply coercive ingredients to restrict the right and suppress the growth of religious competitors with threats and intimidation. This implies that if what the government is doing is called regulation, then these bodies only issue guidelines to limit the enjoyment of the right to freedom of religion in an unlawful manner through the use of force and intimidation. This cannot be regulation. For example, the Nigerian Constitution allows the state legitimately to derogate from the right to freedom of religion through laws that are "reasonably justifiable in a democratic society" on the grounds of defence, public safety, public order, public morality and public health and for the purpose of protecting the rights of others.[17] Also, Article 18(3) of the International Covenant on Civil and Political Rights (ICCPR) contains a similar provision. Bodies other than the government do not have this power in law. In summary, government can legitimately regulate under section 45 of the Nigerian Constitution or Article 18(3) of the ICCPR while other bodies can only issue guidelines which bind their members because they do not have regulatory power under the law.

Third, it cancels out the state motive behind every regulation of freedom of religion. State practice in some orders indicates that every regulation of freedom of religion is a reflection, protection and an advancement of a particular ideology in society, whether religious or non-religious. When the state regulates freedom of religion, it does so for a benefit; to protect its secular status, whatever that means, and if that is true, the action may qualify as a reflection, protection and advancement of that particular ideology. If it is done in order to protect a dominant religious ideology or satisfy the yearnings and aspirations of members of a dominant religious group then the action may qualify as a reflection, protection and advancement of the ideology of that dominant religion. In addition, political benefit may be envisaged here. The idea of motive behind the regulation of religions may extend to noting differences in a country's political, economic and religious context.[18]

17 Constitution of the Federal Republic of Nigeria, 1999, s. 45.

18 See Anthony Gill, Religious Pluralism, Political Incentives, and the Origins of Religious Liberty, in Allen D. Hertzke(ed), *The Future of Religious Freedom: Global Challenges*, (Oxford University Press, Oxford, 2013), pp. 107–127.

In view of the foregoing therefore, a definition of regulation in this context must take these issues into account to avoid ambiguity. The focus of this research is on a collaborative form of regulation of freedom of religion, and for that purpose, regulation of freedom of religion means the enactment of laws, the introduction of policies or other administrative measures by the government or its agents suo motu as in a secular regime or in collaboration with dominant religious groups in the state to restrict citizens' right to enjoy all or any aspect of freedom of religion in the state the aim of which is for the government to gain political support or some other benefit in return from the dominant religious group.

The next concept is the phrase "democratic society." The Nigerian Constitution provides in section 45 that the state may derogate from freedom of religion, among other rights, in a prescribed manner through a law that is "reasonably justifiable in a democratic society" on the grounds of "defence", "public safety", "public order", "public morality" and "public health" and for the purpose of "protecting the rights of others." The Constitution did not however define the phrase. Nigerian courts have also not given any explanation of the meaning of the phrase, which necessitated looking elsewhere[19] to understand its meaning. In order to define it for the purpose of this research, it should be noted first that the functions of government as an institutional framework of control and governance revolve around three major activities, namely "making laws, implementing laws and adjudicating disputes and interpretation of laws".[20] It is therefore important to start by identifying the underlying principles of the phrase as defined in some other jurisdictions such as that of the European Court of Human Rights (ECtHR). The principles are fairness, transparency and equitable representation, the aim of which is to salvage yearnings and objectives of people via public policy, legislation and political stability.

In this sense of the phrase the government is expected to be neutral in its dealings with its people. The ECtHR emphasised this role in the management of religious groups in the case of *Hasan and Chaush* v. *Bulgaria*. In this case, the court held that where the state fails to be detached in the exercise of its powers, the failure can be interpreted to mean tampering with the citizens' right to manifest their religion. The court adopted the same approach in the case of *Metropolitan Church of Bessarabia* v. *Moldova*.[21] In this case, the Moldovan

---

19 *Ogugu* v. *State* [1998] 1 HRLRA 167,189 (SC).

20 Nwanolue B. & Ezenwaobi, O, "Legislative Policies and Citizens Welfarism in the 21st Century Nigerian Polity: The Political Economy Approach", Department of Political Science, 2013.

21 *Metropolitan Church of Bessarabia and others* v. *Moldova* (2002) 35 EHRR, 306 para. 116. 91.

authorities refused the application of a Church for official recognition and without recognition, the Church and the actions of its members would be rendered unlawful. The court held that the state has an obligation to remain non-aligned whenever it is exercising its power to regulate and also in its relations with religions and denominations existing under its authority. And any evidence that the state has failed to act in such a manner in its dealings with religious bodies will require justification under Article 9 (2) if it is not to amount to a breach of Article 9.

The court took the same line in other cases such as *Kokkinakis* v. *Greece*[22] and *Larrisis and Others* v. *Greece*. It emphasised the role of the state in providing the environment enabling them to practise their religion without any form of hindrance from any quarter. This decision added more on the role of the state to remain even-handed in its management of religions and believers in its domain.The impartiality requirement means that the state should have no interest at all in the internal matters of religious organisations unless it is clear that such matters, if allowed, would endanger public order, health, morals and the rights and freedom of others.

For example, in the case of *Serif v. Greece*,[23] the court held that "in democratic societies the state does not need to take measures to ensure that religious communities are brought under a unified leadership." Such an approach casts the role of the state as a "facilitator" of organisational and individual religious freedom. An alternative model, which seems to be the dominant model now, takes a different approach, emphasising the responsibility of the state to ensure the realisation of all Conventional rights, emphasising the need for the freedom of religion and belief to be understood in the broader context of democratic society. In the *Kokkinakis* case, the court held that "the freedom of thought, conscience and religion is one of the foundations of a democratic society....". It also said that "in democratic societies ... it may be necessary to place restrictions on this freedom in order to reconcile the interests of the various groups and ensure that everyone's beliefs are respected."

Another cardinal principle of a democratic society is pluralism. If the state is detached in its dealings with religious groups, then that will have the practical effect of fostering a climate of pluralism and tolerance. However, there are issues to consider here. Religions generally promote absolutist truth claims such as in the case of *Serif* v. *Greece* where the applicant argued that his conviction after he had taken over the functions of the leader of the Muslim community

22 *Kokkinakis* v. *Greece* (14307/88) 1993. 92 Judgment of 24/2/1998, RJD-1998-1, 23 EHHR 329.

23 *Serif* v. *Greece*, no. 38178/97, para. 52, ECHR 1999-IX. 94; *Kokkinakis* v. *Greece* (14307/88) 1993, paras 31 and 33.

in Rodopi which was in dispute was a violation of his freedom of religion. The court held that even though it recognises that tension may be created in situations where there is an internal rift within a religious community, it however considers that such a rift is an unavoidable consequence of pluralism which should at best be tolerated by the state through some mechanisms.

In such circumstances it is not for the state to eliminate pluralism because it causes tension; the state should rather devise ways in which the contending parties can tolerate one another. The state can achieve this by exercising some form of oversight function over the internal affairs of religious communities in the interests of ensuring pluralism and tolerance, but without tampering with the autonomy of that religious community. The state must demonstrate its non-aligned status in this regard. The court clarified this role in the case of *Metropolitan Church of Bessarabia* v. *Moldova* when it rejected the government's argument opposing the recognition of the Church as a legal entity because doing so, according to it, would widen the crack within the Orthodox community. The court held that the "state's duty of neutrality ... is incompatible with any power ... to assess the legitimacy of religious beliefs, and requires the state to ensure that conflicting groups tolerate each other, even when they originated in the same group."

This might be contrasted with the case of the *Supreme Holy Council of the Muslim Community v. Bulgaria*,[24] in which the court placed more emphasis on the role of the state as the promoter of tolerance. In both the *Metropolitan Church of Bessarabia* case and the *97 Members of the Gladini Congregation* case, the Court emphasised that neutrality cannot be used to justify a failure to protect the rights of believers under Article 9.

Debates on the Regulation of Freedom of Religion

Religious propagation is a component of freedom of religion. And its regulation means the exercise of state regulatory power to limit citizens' rights to enjoy freedom of religion or, more specifically, restricting citizens' right to enage in religious propagation using laws that are supposedly reasonable and justifiable in a democratic society based on the assumption that that is being done in the interest of defence, public safety, public order, public morality or public health, and in order to protect the rights and freedom of others.[25] It is in the exercise of this constitutional power, otherwise called the state regulatory

24 15 Hum. Rts. Case Dig. 503(2004–2005).

25 Constitution of the Federal Republic of Nigeria, 1999, s. 45(1).

power, that Kano, Borno and Kaduna States enacted their religious preaching board laws to control this component of freedom of religion called religious preaching in their spheres of influence. Debates on the use of state regulatory power to restrict citizens' right to enagage in religious persuation in democratic orders can be approached from five different perspectives using a wide range of methodologies.

First, American constitutional law experts Audrey Peltze[26] and Kenneth Lasson[27] argue in favour of the regulation of freedom of religion because of the perceived incivility and incitement that religious persuasion includes. Peltze's work, for example, argues that the state can restrict the right to religious preaching, so long as it is done through neutral laws that support government interests while preserving citizens' free exercise of their rights. How can this be achieved? And through what balancing mechanism? These questions are largely unanswered in the theory that Peltze and Lasson describe.

Second, American experts on the regulation of religion such as Brian J. Grim and Roger Finke,[28] along with experts on religion and politics such as Monica Duffy Toft, Daniel Philpot and Timothy Samuel Shah,[29] argue that it is unreasonable and unwise to place restrictions on citizens' rights to freedom of religion in a democracy, because doing so has grave consequences. These works also focus on the religious economy thesis, which posits that in a free market of ideas, religious ideas should be allowed to compete with one another in the available public space so that in the end the truth prevails. Grim and Finke's work in particular demonstrates that most restrictions placed on the right to freedom of religion in democracies are a result of collaboration between the state and dominant religious groups to suppress minority religious groups.[30]

The suppression of minority groups is a practice which should be discouraged. There are relevant scholarly works in Nigeria to support this point. For example, Nigerian historians Auwal Anwar and Haruna Wakili argue that dominant Islamic groups in collaboration with governments in Kaduna and Kano States acted on the pretext of controlling religious preaching to repress

26 Peltze, A., "A Survey of Constitutional Challenges to Municipal Regulation of Religious Solicitation and a Suggested Legislative Compromise", FORDHAM Urban L.J. 1982, 11: 845.

27 Lasson, K., "Incitement in the Mosques: Testing the Limits of Free Speech and Religious Liberty", Whittier L. Rev. 2005, 27:3–59.

28 Grim, B.J., and Finke, R., *The Price of Freedom Denied*, Cambridge University Press, New York, 2011.

29 Toft, M.D., Philpott, D. and Shah, T.S., *God's Century: Resurgent Religion and Global Politics*, W.W. Norton & Company London, 2011.

30 Grim and Finke, *The Price of Freedom Denied*, pp. 25–30.

minority Islamic groups that they regarded as dissidents.[31] These works are relevant and evidence-based in support of their thesis, but none of them provides any particular balancing mechanism to test the reasonableness or otherwise of laws enacted to restrict the right to freedom of religion of the citizens in a democracy. None of them applies a legal approach to the study of the phenomenon. Grim and Finke are engaged in empirical sociological research. Toft and colleagues also write from the perspective of political science.

Third, Nigeria-based legal practitioners such as Sam Amadi and Inibehe Effiong argue that the state should not regulate religious preaching at all—despite the provision of section 45 of the Nigerian Constitution which clearly allows the state to derogate from such rights on the basis of defence, public order, public morality and other factors.[32] Their studies were done in response to Kaduna State's effort to amend the Kaduna State Regulation of Religious Preaching of 1996.[33] For example, Effiong's argument through Nigerian constitutional law is that some specific sections of the Religious Preaching Bill offend provisions of the Nigerian Constitution, particularly section 10 on the prohibition of the adoption of a state religion by any state in the country, Section 38 on freedom of religion and section 45, which allows the state to limit or derogate from these rights. Effiong does not, however, acknowledge the fact that the freedom of religion clause in the Nigerian Constitution is not an absolute right.

A fourth area of scholarship is the one that uses balancing mechanisms or proportionality tests to resolve conflicts between the regulatory power of the state and the right to religious freedom of its citizens. International Law such as the ICCPR proposes a "three-step" standard of judicial review designed to strike a balance between state regulatory power and citizens' freedom of religion in a democratic society.[34] The three-step balancing mechanism requires that for any limitation on freedom of religion to be legitimate in a democratic society it must satisfy these three standards: the prescribed by law requirement, the furtherance of a legitimate state interest qualification and the requirement of proportionality. American constitutional law scholar Jeremy

31 Anwar, A.A., *Gardawa, ulama and the State of Northern Nigeria: The Maitatsine phenomenon (1962–1985.*, Ph.D. Diss., University of Maiduguri, 1998). See also Wakili, H., *The Phenomenon of Revolts and Riots in Kano, 1983–1995: An Historical Perspective* (Ph.D. Diss., Bayero University Kano, 1997).

32 See: Constitution of the Federal Republic of Nigeria 1999, s. 45(1).

33 Kaduna State Regulation of Religious Preaching (Amendment) Edict No. 6 of 1996.

34 These three standards are provided for under Art.18 (3) of the International Convention on Civil and Political Rights (ICCPR). See also European Convention on Human Rights, Art. 9.2, which is similar to the provisions of the ICCPR.

Gunn, however, questions the adequacy of the three-legged standard of review which is notorious in resolving conflicts between the two competing rights.

His argument is that the test lacks guiding principles on the kind of evidence to admit, on which of the two rights is more important than the other and why, and on which of the parties as between the state and the citizen the burden of proving what evidence lies and why.[35] Gunn therefore recommends four standards of review instead of three. According to him, a tribunal faced with the task of interpreting derogatory clauses with respect to freedom of religion should, first, understand its role; second, properly identify the burden of proof of each of the parties; third, apply the less restrictive alternatives with the correct evidentiary obligations placed on both parties; and fourthly, understand the relevant degree of scrutiny to apply.[36]

Gunn's argument, however, negates the role of the overall religion-state pattern, especially in a country like Nigeria, as a guiding principle in the interpretation of freedom of religion cases, as evidenced elsewhere in this work. This relationship is relevant when assessing the nature of the protection of freedom of religion in a country, especially since that religion is indispensable to the maintenance of public order. Particularly in the case of Nigeria, Gunn's fourth recommendation raises the question of how to determine the relevant degree of scrutiny. And this is where the main problem is. What degree of scrutiny should be applied in striking a balance between state regulatory power and freedom of religion? How? Why?

Addressing these questions is particularly important in Nigeria. This is because the Nigerian Constitution happily protects a citizen's right to "freedom of thought, conscience, religion or belief and freedom (either alone or in community with others, and in public or in private) to manifest and propagate his religion or belief in worship, teaching and observance."[37] The Constitution also protects "freedom of expression, including freedom to hold opinions and to receive and impart ideas and information without interference" and to "assemble freely" and "associate with others."[38] As law and religion scholar W. Cole

35 Gunn, T.J., "Permissible Limitations on Freedom of Religion or Belief", in Witte, J. (Jr) and Green, M.C. (eds). *Religion and Human Rights: An Introduction*, Oxford University Press, Oxford, 2011, pp. 263–264.

36 *Ibid*, p. 266.

37 Constitution of the Federal Republic of Nigeria, s. 38 (1).

38 Constitution of the Federal Republic of Nigeria, ss. 39 and 40.

Durham Jr. has observed, freedom of religion is a "core doctrine" amongst other fundamental human rights in the world today.[39]

However, the Nigerian Constitution also allows the state to derogate from these rights when "reasonably justifiable in a democratic society" on the grounds of "defence, public safety, public order, public morality, public health" and for the purpose of "protecting the rights of others."[40] The Constitution, however, does not define the phrase "democratic society", the criteria for its determination, or what qualifies a law to be "reasonably justifiable" in a society such as Nigeria. The lack of definition creates a legal normative space that ought to be filled either by the court through the exercise of discretion in the event of conflict between the two competing rights, or by the legislature through the enactment of the law. A solution to this definitional dilemma requires the application of a suitable balancing mechanism or proportionality assessment technique to understand the meaning of the phrases which this works seeks to provide.

An Overview of the Regulation of Religious Preaching in Northern Nigeria

History

The regulation of religious preaching, Islamic religious preaching specifically, is an old phenomenon in Northern Nigeria.[41] However, the way in which it evolved in the states of what is now called Northern Nigeria indicates two of its features in all the states. First, it was always discriminatory against minority religious groups in favour of established religious groups in the region. Second, the preaching laws are designed to silence dissent in the competition for space with a view to favouring dominant religious groups and to help them consolidate their positions in the religious market place. Historically, the attempt by the king of Gobir, Bawa Jan Gwarzo, in the late eighteenth century to control the Islamic religious preaching of Usman dan Fodio before the launching of the latter's jihad may probably be the first effort to regulate religious preaching

39 See Durham W.C. (Jr)., "Perspectives on Religious Liberty: A Comparative Framework," in van der Vyver, J.D., and Witte, J. (eds), *Religious Human Rights Global Perspective*, Martinus Nijhoff, Boston, 2011, pp. 1–44.

40 Constitution of the Federal Republic of Nigeria, s. 45.

41 Gwandu, A., "Aspects of the Administration of Justice in the Sokoto Caliphate and Shaykh Abdullahi ibn Fodio's Contribution to it," in Rashid, K.S., (ed.), *Islamic Law in Nigeria*, (Kaduna: Islamic Publications Bureau, 1986), pp. 10–27.

in the region.[42] After King Bawa's death, his brother King Nafata continued along the same lines but more strictly; he restricted Islamic religious preaching in the land of Gobir,[43] barred people not born to Muslim families from converting to Islam[44] and ordered all proselytes to renounce Islam and go back to their traditional religion.[45] He also proscribed the wearing of turbans and veils by men and women respectively.[46] Usman dan Fodio ignored the king's orders, and this confrontation ended in the well-known jihad beginning in 1804.[47] The success of the jihad gave rise to a new administration with Usman dan Fodio as the leader. He then appointed emirs as his deputies in many parts of today's Northern Nigeria, including places such as Sokoto, Zaria, Kano and Nupeland.[48]

The second attempt to regulate Islamic preaching took place under the colonial administration in 1926, as a reaction to incessant disagreements between the dominant Islamic religious groups in the region. These conflicts were essentially between the *Qadiriyya* and *Tijjaniyya Sufi* orders, in addition to the friction associated with the emergence of new Islamic religious groups such as the *Ahmadiyya* and the *Wahhabiyya* in the region.[49] Moreover, at that time, the region had witnessed a rise in the number of Christian religious missionaries who were struggling to win more souls for Christianity against the wishes of the northern emirs, who were Muslims.[50]As a result, the colonial government issued a circular directing the resident governors of Kano, Zaria, Sokoto and Niger to issue proclamations to control religious preaching generally in their areas in order to avoid any possible infringement of law and order.[51]

42 Laremont, R.R., *Islamic Law and Politics in Northern Nigeria*, New Jersey: Africa World Press, 2011, pp. 64–65.

43 Ibid.

44 Ibid.

45 Ibid.

46 Ibid.

47 Ibid.

48 For details of the atrocities committed by Hausa Kings before Jihad see Uthman b. Fodio, *Kitab al-Faraq*, trans. M. Hisket, in *Bulletin of the School of Oriental and African Studies* (BSOAS),(London, 1960) XXIII, 3. See also Mohammed, B., *Infaq al-Mansur*, ed. C.E.J. Whiting (London, 1957), p. 65.

49 Wakili, H., "The Phenomenon of Revolts and Riots in Kano, 1893–1995" (Ph.D diss., unpublished, Bayero University Kano, 1997), pp. 38–45.

50 Afolayan, F., "Religion and Politics in Colonial Nigeria: The Life and Career of Sir Walter Miller, 1782–1952," in Julius, O. Adekunle, *Religion in Politics: Secularism and National Integration in Modern Nigeria*, New Jersey Inc.: Africa World Press, 2009, pp. 37–66.

51 Middleton, H.H., *Memorandum to Residents; Kano, Zaria, Sokoto and Niger*. Missionary Activities in Muslim Centres, 13 December, 1926.

All residents complied with this directive. For example, the proclamation of the Emir of Kano at the time, Abdullahi Bayero, reads as follows (author's translation):

> From Emir of Kano Abdullahi Bayero.
>
> Salutations to the people of the whole land of Kano, District Heads, Village Heads and peasantry, religious scholars and the entire male and female population of the land, as well as to the strangers inhabiting the jurisdiction. Know that this is a decree from us to you. Let no man amongst you preach, no matter who he may be, in a city, on a road, or in towns, or in wards of towns, or in hamlets or villages. Whosoever wishes to preach, let him go to his mosque to preach there. Or let him preach in his house. Whoever shall disobey this decree and does what we have forbidden, let him blame no one but himself for what will befall him. Written in friendship on Friday the 3rd of Rajab, 1345 AH (7 January 1927).[52]

This was the situation up to 1950, and then through 1960 when Nigeria became independent and gained a new Constitution. That constitution for the first time provided the people with full liberal rights including freedoms of religion, expression and association.[53]

A third attempt to control religious preaching, however, occurred soon afterwards, and it was designed to control minority religious groups called Gardawa perceived as dissidents in the region by authorities in favour of the dominant *sufi* religious groups. Major sources of conflict between some Gardawa and people in the early 1960s among other things were their denunciation of *Tasawwuf* and the *sufi* brotherhoods as well as their opposition to the use of Hadith and other related books of the Shari'ah besides the Qur'an.[54] Their various open air preaching patterns were popularly called *Wa'azin Turmi* (preaching while seated on a bench-like stool made from tree branches) which is specifically associated with the Muhammadu Marwa Gardawa group, *Wa'azin Fitilar Ruwa*

52 The writer acquired copies of these documents from Dr. Philip Ostien while working as his research assistant on the documentation of the sharia project in Northern Nigeria from 2005 to 2007. Dr. Ostien was formerly based at the Faculty of Law, University of Jos and the writer was his student from 1998 to 2004 in the same faculty. Other emirs of the areas have done the same thing. The Emir of Zaria issued his circular on 12 January 1927 while the emir of Katsina issued his own on 26 August 1927. Also see Lethem, J.G., and Memorandum to Resident Province, Preaching in Public Places, 4 January 1930. Also see Auwal, A., pp. 88–90.

53 See Chapter IV of the Constitution of the Federal Republic of Nigeria 1999 as amended.

54 Auwal, A., *Gardawa, Ulama and the State in Northern Nigeria: The Maitatsine Phenomenon, 1962–1985*, Ph.D. diss., unpublished, University of Maiduguri (1997), p. 102.

(preaching with the aid of a lantern), *Wa'azin Kasuwa* (preaching at the market place) and *Wa'azin Kan Hanya* (preaching by the *road side*).[55]

Wa'azin Gardawa has some features that distinguish it from other forms of religious preaching. First, their interpretation is a product of speculation. Second, they use incorrect Hausa interpretations to misrepresent the actual meanings of the Qur'anic verses they use in their preaching sessions.[56] Third, they indoctrinate their followers and do not welcome rational thinking. They do not entertain question and answer sessions during or at the end of their preaching sessions unless such questions accord with their way of reasoning.[57]

Leaders of the *sufi* brotherhoods in Kano capitalised on these trends in gardawa as the basis for their collaboration with the governments of the various states in the Northern region to persecute and terminate the religious activities of *gardawa* in the religious market place. The consequequence of their collaboration became obvious between 1962 and 1975. For example, the Fityanul Islam Organisation, the political wing of the Tijjaniyya sufi order in Nigeria, protested against the preaching of *gardawa* on 7 January 1964 in a petition they presented to the premier of the Northern Region; Sir Ahmadu Sardauna of Sokoto.[58] They demanded that the activities of road preachers such as the *gardawa* be forbidden in all the provinces until the Premier established a committee of competent *ulama* that would scrutinise them and certify them as fit and proper to engage in Islamic religious preaching.[59] The premier did not respond to them at the initial stage and they wrote to him again on 25 July 1964. But this time around, they directed their letter to the Committee of Ulama established by the Premier of the Northern Region on 23 August 1963 to unite the different Islamic groups in the region.[60]

In reaction, the Sardauna issued a circular to all the Northern provinces, directing them to make the possession of a preaching licence a condition precedent for Islamic religious preachers before they were allowed to preach in the region.[61] This was a sort of "*de facto*" religious regulation through the indirect influence of the dominant religious groups in the region. That measure forced the *Gardawa* off the preaching scene for about two years and on the other hand favoured the dominant religious groups in the religious open market place.

55 Ibid., at 103.
56 Ibid., at 109.
57 Ibid.
58 Ibid., at 103.
59 Ibid., at 104.
60 Ibid.
61 Ibid., at 104.

Although the Sardauna belonged to the *Qadiriyya* Islamic religious group and his actions impacted negatively on the *Gardawa* group, research however indicates that he was liberal and ecumenical in matters of religion until he was killed in the military coup of 1966.[62]

The *Gardawa* resurfaced in 1969 in Kano towards the end of the Nigerian civil war and continued to preach without a licence.[63] The *ulama* in Kano state, which consisted of members of the dominant *Sufi* orders, sought the intervention of the government through the Emir of Kano on the need to regulate the Islamic religious preaching of the *gardawa*, which effort culminated in the enactment of the first legislative instrument on Islamic religious preaching in the state and Northern Nigeria at large, as would be seen later. The paper considers this to be the fourth attempt to regulate Islamic religious preaching in the region.

Then *Izala*, a *Wahhabi*-oriented Islamic religious group close to Sheikh Abubakar Gumi which was strongly opposed to *Sufi* doctrines and practices, emerged on the scene in 1978.[64] The emergence of *Izala* changed the equation of Muslim intra-religious conflict in Northern Nigeria from *Qadiriyya* vs. *Tijaniyya* to *Tariqa* (i.e. *Qadiriyya* and *Tijaniyya* collectively) vs. *Izala*. *Izala* immediately began a campaign of offensive preaching directed against *Sufi* doctrines, which it labelled *bid'a* (heretical innovation) and *shirk* (polytheism). In their preaching, *Izala* preachers openly mentioned the personal names of the founders of *Sufi* orders. They engaged in *Takfir* and even divorced their mosques from those of the *Sufi* orders, as they did not allow their members to follow an imam affiliated to a *Sufi* order. This led to a series of skirmishes between the two groups.[65]

While the imbroglio between the *Izala* and *Tariqa* groups continued, some of the disgruntled *Gardawa* re-emerged on the scene under the form of the *'Yan Tatsine*; these were the followers of Muhammadu Marwa Maitatsine, a peripatetic preacher from northern Cameroon who had settled in Kano where he had engaged in belligerent public preaching against all the existing Islamic groups in the region.[66] *Maitatsine*'s doctrines were different from those of both *Izala* and *Tariqa*. For example, while both *Izala* and *Tariqa* accepted the *Qur'an*

62 Kuka, M.H., *Religion, Power and Politics in Northern Nigeria* (Ibadan: Spectrum Books Limited, 2011), pp. ix–xiii.

63 Auwal, A., *Gardawa, Ulama and the State in Northern Nigeria: The Maitatsine Phenomenon, 1962–1985* (Ph.D diss., unpublished, University of Maiduguri, 1997), p. 84.

64 Ibid.

65 Ibid.

66 Ibid.

and the *Hadith* as dependable sources of divine revelation, and the *Sunni* jurisprudential tradition (*Fiqh*) as a valid body of interpretation, *Maitatsine* discarded all except the *Qur'an*. In 1980, the *Maitatsine* movement engaged in a militant uprising in Kano State. The ensuing military operation left thousands dead, and public opinion in the country became increasingly supportive of the need to regulate religious preaching.

Although there were Preaching Board laws in most of the states of Northern Nigeria including Kano state, the civilian administration of President Shehu Shagari decided to ban open-air preaching instead of applying the existing laws in the state. This decision especially burdened *Izala*, as open-air Islamic religious preaching was their main preaching technique.

Military officers headed by Major General Muhammadu Buhari toppled the civilian administration in 1983. This regime took a cue from the past civilian administration and placed a "blanket ban on religious activities especially open-air preaching."[67] In addition, it forbade the building of new Friday mosques without the permission of emirate authorities. In order to prevent preachers from circumventing any ban imposed by the Preaching Board committee of a particular emirate by applying to a neighbouring one, the Government also introduced a requirement according to which authorisation for religious preaching must be obtained both in the preacher's emirate of origin as well as in any other emirate where he might wish to preach. As most of the Preaching Boards were constituted by scholars affiliated to the *Sufi* orders, which at the time represented most of the country's religious scholars, *Izala* found the new measures to be burdensome. Because of this, the founder of *Izala*, the late Shaykh Ismaila Idiris, was reported to have said in one of his preaching sessions, after both regimes were out of office, that "Allah will not forgive the regimes of Shagari and that of Buhari because they blocked the way of Allah."[68]

Another military junta, led by General Ibrahim Badamasi Babangida, took power in 1985. Preaching Board laws remained unchanged in the various states. This government, however, became more liberal in its attitude towards religious groups generally. In 1987, it enacted a law establishing an advisory council on religious affairs to handle issues of religion in the country. It is not clear, however, to what extent this body was actually useful. In the early 1990s, *Izala* split into two factions, one linked to the group's older leadership based in Jos, with the other linked to the group's new leadership based in Kaduna. This

67 Sani, M.U., "Changing Islamic Identity in Nigeria from the 1960s to the 1980s: From Sufism to anti Sufism", in Brenner, I., (ed.), *Muslim Identity and Social Change in Sub-Saharan Africa*) (Bloomington and Indianapolis: Indiana University Press, 1993), pp. 154–178.

68 Ibid.

split further changed the nature of the intra-Muslim conflict from *Tariqa* vs. *Izala* to "Jos *Izala*" vs. "Kaduna *Izala*." Apart from minor skirmishes here and there between members of the two factions of *Izala* and sometimes between *Izala* (Jos-based and Kaduna-based) and members of *Tariqa*, no other major conflict occurred in Northern Nigeria as a result of government regulation of religious preaching until 2009, when it arose in Borno State between members of the *Boko Haram* and the government of Nigeria, which event led to the extra-judicial killing of the group's leader; Mohammad Yusuf and many of his members and other citizens of Nigeria.

Changes

It is pertinent to point out that the regulation of religious preaching by means of legislative enactment, as in the case of Kano, brought a new dimension to the scope of the regulation. Before 1970, only one Northern region exists as a whole with its components. The pattern of regulation was not by legislative enactment, but by the Premier's executive fiat and often times done with the support of dominant Islamic religious groups in the region. In addition, the regulation was meant for application in all the components of the region as a whole. After the civil war (1967–1970), however, the three regions that used to constitute the Federal Republic of Nigeria were sub-divided into smaller states. Kano became one of the newly established states in this new arrangement in the defunct Northern Nigeria. It enacted its own law for the regulation of Islamic preaching, as seen above and became the first state to do so in the whole of the Northern region. Borno state followed suit in 1977, then Niger and Sokoto states in 1979 and Bauchi state in 1984. These states subsequently amended their preaching laws, with the exception of Bauchi which suspended its own and instead banned open-air preaching. Plateau and Katsina states enacted their preaching laws in 1986 and 1991 respectively. From 1990 to 1996, the new states of Jigawa, Kebbi, Yobe, Zamfara, Gombe and Nassarawa were created within the territory of the former region of Northern Nigeria, and all of them inherited the religious preaching laws of their mother states. It should be noted that most of the Preaching Board laws were initially the product of military regimes in consultation with local interest groups and were not the product of constitutional democratic processes. The only exceptions were the following:

a) Borno State's two Islamic Religious Preaching Board laws (the 1981 law and its 2010 amendment);
b) Kano State's Council for Islamic Affairs Law (1981), subsequently repealed and replaced by the Religious Preaching Edict (1985);

c) Kaduna State Religious Preaching Edict No. 7 of 1984 has been the preaching law in the state. It was amended by the Regulation of Religious Preaching (Amendment) Edicts No. 1 of 1987 and No. 6 of 1996 respectively. The state is currently making an effort to amend its preaching edict through the introduction of the Kaduna State Religious Preaching Bill 2016 which is now being debated;
d) Zamfara State's Religious Preaching and Establishment of Juma'at Mosque and Idi Praying Ground Commission Law (2003);
e) Kebbi State's Preaching Law (2004);
f) Katsina State's Islamic Education and Preaching Law (2011), although that is yet to be passed;
g) Jigawa State's Religious Preaching Law, amended by Law No. 14 of 2012;
h) The Niger State's Religious Preaching and Place of Worship (Amendment) Bill 2013. This bill is presently among the pending bills in the state.[69]

Kano, Borno and Kaduna States

In this section, the religious preaching laws of Kano, Borno and Kaduna States will be treated together. The aim is to understand the circumstances under which each was enacted, the role of the dominant religious groups in the enactment and the implications for freedom of religion. The religious preaching laws of Kano and Borno States are designed specifically to regulate Islamic religious preaching. That of Kaduna State, on the other hand, is intended to regulate Islamic and Christian religious preaching. But one obvious general feature that all the preaching board laws of the various states possessed is the function that mandates the boards to examine intending religious preachers, to issue preaching licences to those qualified, and to criminalise preaching without a licence or in contravention of its content. In terms of spread, these laws are found in thirteen (13) states in Northern Nigeria, eleven (11) of which are the states that enacted various shari'a-related legislation as part of their shari'a implementation programmes. They are Kano, Jigawa, Borno, Yobe, Bauchi, Gombe, Sokoto, Zamfara, Kebbi, Niger, Kaduna, Katsina, Plateau and Nassarawa States. The religious preaching laws are designed to regulate Islamic religious preaching with the exception of those of Bauchi, Plateau, Nassarawa and Kaduna states. It is shown elsewhere that the composition of the Islamic

69 The Attorney General of Niger State revealed this fact during an interview session I and Dr. Philip Ostein had with him in his office on 25 January 2016.

religious preaching boards is determined by the governments of the states, and in practice such compositions have mainly favoured dominant religious groups over minority religious groups, as shown in the discourse below.

Kano

Long before 1967, when the civil war broke out in Nigeria, and particularly from 1961, Kano's emirate and dominant religious groups were disturbed by the religious preaching of *gardawa*, most of whom also engage in the interpretation of the Qur'an during Ramadan (the fasting period). These are people such as Muhammadu Marwa alais Maitatsine, Lawal Kalarawi, Yahaya Maidal, Maizabura, Maidankokoa, Turnuku, Maitsagewa, Salihi Faki (or Dankadabere), Uba Yakasai, Audu Nafada, Usman Waqad Ja'al haq, Idris Sokoto, Usman Gano, Danzakara and Maikaulasan.[70] For example sometime in 1962 the authorities in Kano accused Muhammadu Marwa alias Maitatsine of using offensive language during his religious preaching sessions against accepted religious beliefs, practices, institutions and leaders, which culminated in his arrest, trial and subsequent deportation on the orders of the Emir of Kano, Sir Muhammadu Sunusi.[71] He returned to Kano State in 1963 after the deposition of Sir Muhammad Sunusi as the emir of Kano. Indeed an expert in the history of Islamic legal education in Kano, John Weir Chamberlin, observed that:

> Tafsir was sometimes used for thinly-veiled political commentary. In recent years, Kano's local government has sought to control the potential for political commentary by demanding that everyone intending to present tafsir during Ramadan pass a test on knowledge of the Qur'an. The government has administered the test.[72]

To address the problem the Emir of Kano designed some rules called the Kano Local Government Area Quranic Interpretation and Admonishing Rules which

70 Auwal, A., *Gardawa, Ulama and the State in Northern Nigeria: The Maitatsine Phenomenon, 1962–1985*, Ph.D diss., unpublished, University of Maiduguri, (1997), p. 103.

71 The deportation of Maitatsine is shrouded in confusion. It is not clear from scholarly works whether his deportation complied with the law. How he was deported is not also clear. It is not, however, in dispute that he was at least forced to leave Kano at least for a year.

72 Chamberlin, J.W., *The Development of Islamic Education in Kano City, Nigeria, With Emphasis on Legal Education in the 19th and 20th Centuries* (Ph.D diss., Columbia University 1975), p. 168.

became public on 4 September 1967.[73] But possibly because of the civil war that broke out in 1967, nothing happened because *gardawa* had vanished from the scene. They re-emerged towards the end of the war in 1969 and continued preaching without a licence in Kano. In reaction the sufi brotherhood's ulama in Kano persuaded the emir of Kano to talk to the Governor of Kano State, Alhaji Audu Bako, about the need to design social control measures against *gardawa* religious preachers to avoid a possible breakdown of law and order in the state. The Governor later authorised the emir to establish a Committee of ten Islamic scholars to screen intending Islamic religious preachers in the state and certify them as fit and proper before they were allowed to engage in public religious preaching or Qur'anic translation.

In line with the Governor's directive the emir formed a committee comprising leading scholars from the dominant Sufi orders in the state. This committee included Shaykh Nasiru Kabara (d. 1996), Shaykh Tijani Usman (d. 1970), Shehu Maihula (d. 1988) and Shaykh Sani Kafanga (d. 1989). The composition of the committee made it clear that the emir was influenced by members of the dominant sufi brotherhoods in forming the committee. It also left nobody in any doubt that it was targeted against the minority *gardawa* religious preachers in the state.[74]

This was evidenced in their mode of operation. The committee first formed a supervisory committee consisting of their followers to act as secret agents to detect members of the gardawa group with a view to identifying those preaching without a licence or those preaching in contravention of the rules of preaching set out in the preaching permit. The police collaborated with this supervisory committee to check the activities of the gardawa in Kano[75]. At the end of the day, the committee of ten denied the gardawa a licence to preach in Kano.

Anwar reported that Shaikh Dahiru Bauchi; a well respected member of the Tijjaniyya sufi brotherhood from Tijjaniyya, reported on the encounter between Muhammadu Marwa alias Maitatsine and this committee of experts in Kano sometime in 1967. He stated that Maitatsine appeared before the committee but his performance was nothing to write home about and he was denied a licence to preach.[76] Even though Shaikh Dahiru Bauchi is highly respected, the fact that he was not a member of the committee of experts before whom

---

73 Auwal, A., *Gardawa, Ulama and the State in Northern Nigeria: The Maitatsine Phenomenon, 1962–1985* (Ph.D diss., unpublished, University of Maiduguri, 1997), p. 107.

74 Ibid., at 264.

75 Ibid., at 105.

76 Ibid., at 119.

Maitatsine appeared calls the probative value of his report into question. In addition, as a sufi himself, Shaikh Dahiru Bauchi was a member of the forces fighting Maitatsine. So the report is similar to a rat appearing before a cat for justice. Because of the committee's denial of preaching licence for them, the gardawa tactfully withrew from the scene.

It is however alleged that they moved to Kaduna and were able to obtain preaching licences from the Jama'atu Nasril Islam, then headed by Shaykh Abubakar Mahmud Gumi who was perceived by members of the sufi brotherhoods as anti-sufi.[77] It was also alleged that even Maitatsine obtained a preaching licence through him despite the latter's poor performance before the interview panel.[78] But Gumi denied issuing a preaching licence to the *gardawa*. He stated that:

> Those I gave permission to preach were scholars not gardawa. You see, there was a lot of politics in Kano. When a preacher did not agree to follow the sufi scholars in their deviation or unbelief, they simply handed him over to police and accuse him of causing disturbances. Most of those who got their preaching permission from Kaduna were tested by the Jama'at Nasril Islam and were found fit. They were not even known to me personally.[79]

Maitatsine and other *gardawa* re-appeared in 1970 and continued with their Islamic religious preaching without a preaching licence in Kano. In reaction, the state revived the emir of Kano's committee of scholars in 1970. The Governor also approved the emir of Kano's proposal called the Kano Local Government Area Quranic Interpretation and Admonishing Rules, designed to control religious preaching in Kano on 1 April 1970, and it became the first edict (legislative enactment) in the state.[80] The law stipulated that whoever enaged in religious preaching without a licence would be sentenced to six months' imprisonment or would be liable to a fine of fifty pounds [£ 50] or both.[81]

77 Auwal, *supra, Gardawa, Ulama and the State in Northern Nigeria: The Maitatsine Phenomenon, 1962–1985*, p. 4.

78 Ibid., at 119.

79 Ibid., at 106.

80 Kano Local Government Authority (Control of Quranic Interpretation and Admonishing) Rules 1970. This became Kano Local Government Law No. 3, 1970.

81 Auwal, *supra, Gardawa, Ulama and the State in Northern Nigeria: The Maitatsine Phenomenon, 1962–1985*, p. 121.

These measures taken by the government of Kano State placed restriction on the religious activities of *gardawa* in the state between 1970 and 1971. As a result, they protested against the enforcement of the Kano State Local Government Authority (Control of Qur'anic Interpretation and Admonishing) Edict, 1970 which banned them from engaging in religious preaching in Kano State. In doing so they attacked the emir of Kano, Alhaji Ado Bayero, at Friday congregational prayers as a result of which more than 40 of their leading figures were arrested by the police and subsequently detained in Port Harcourt in 1973. The repression of *gardawa* by the state in collaboration with the dominant sufi orders put their activities to a halt and those of them that were not arrested became secretive in their operation between 1973 and 1975.[82] Those who were detained were released in 1975 under the regime of General Murtala Ramat Mohammed on the advice of Shaikh Mahmood Gumi. According to Gumi:

> The ulama misled the government to detain them. I got a lot of appeals from people on their behalf, being the Grand Khadi. When we held a National Conferennce for Judges in Lagos, I raised the issue of the ulama of Kano putting innocent preachers in detention. The Chief Judge of Port Harcourt testified that he also saw some of them in Port Harcourt and they all seemed harmless. On the basis of our observations, I requested the meeting to demand for their immediate release and they were all released.[83]

It should be noted that after their release Maitatsine reduced his open-air religious preachings. He concentrated on teaching his ideology to his followers at home. In turn, his followers imparted the ideology to numerous others by means of itinerant open-air religious preaching in Kano, Borno and Kaduna States.[84] The law however continued to operate in the state until section 20 of Kano's Religious Preaching Law of 1985 repealed it along with another law called the Kano State law for the Establishment of the Council for Islamic Affairs, 1982. The existence of this law in Kano state did not stop intra-religious skirmishes between members of Izala and the Tariqa Islamic groups from 1970 to 1980. While the confrontation between the two groups was going on, some members of the gardawa Islamic groups re-emerged on the scene in the form of Yan Tatsine. These were the followers of Muhammadu Marwa Maitatsine,

---

82 Ibid., at 122.

83 Ibid.

84 Ibid., at 124.

a known peripatetic preacher from northern Cameroon who had settled in Kano where he had engaged in belligerent public preaching against all the existing Islamic groups in the region.[85] Maitatsine's doctrines were different from those of both Izala and Tariqa. For example, while both Izala and Tariqa accepted the Qur'an and the Hadith as dependable sources of divine revelation, and the Sunni jurisprudential tradition (Fiqh) as a valid body of interpretation, Maitatsine discarded all except the Qur'an.

In 1980, the Maitatsine movement engaged in a militant uprising in Kano State. Research on the uprising however demonstrates that before it broke out intelligence reports in the state indicated instances of ferocious public Islamic preaching at Friday mosques in the state from July 1973 to 1979 which involved Maitatsine.[86] Tension increased in the state, and in reaction the government sent a written ultimatum to Muhammadu Marwa Maitatsine, the leader of the group, directing him and his followers to leave the area they were occupying within two weeks. This ultimatum angered the group, as a result of which they mobilised themselves and confronted the Government on 18 December 1980.[87] This became the popular Maitatsine riots in Kano State.

The Nigerian Army brought this confrontation under control on 30 December 1980. A critical question to ask at this stage is what happened to the Islamic Preaching Board law in operation in the state? Why did the government of Kano State neglect to apply the law to control the *Izala* and *Tariqa* confrontations and later the violent preaching of Maitatsine against other Islamic religious groups at Friday mosque which, according to reports, became apparent from early 1973?

Analysis of Preaching Laws in Kano 1970–1985

It is stated in the preceding paragraphs that the Kano State Local Government Authority (Control of Qur'anic Interpretation and Admonishing) Edict, 1970 was the first religious preaching law in the state. The main problem in Kano then was the issue of *tafsir* (Qur'anic interpretation) and also religious preaching by *gardawa*. This law was specifically enacted to control this group of people who were perceived by members of dominant Islamic religious groups in Kano as a dissident Islamic group which had to be controlled. Section 1 of the law establishes in all the local government areas of the state committees called

85 Ibid., at 122.

86 Wakili, H., *The Phenomenon of Revolts and Riots in Kano, 1893–1995* (Ph.D diss., unpublished, Bayero University Kano, 1997), pp. 172–173.

87 Ibid.

the Interpretation and Admonishing Committee with membership at the discretion of the heads of the local government councils in the state.

The function of the committees was to issue preaching permits to Islamic preachers who intend to "admonish and/or interpret the Qura'an" in the territory of any of the local government areas. And in 1980 the Maitatsine problem came with more advanced challenges, and in reaction to it the government of Kano State enacted another law called the the Kano State Council for Islamic Affairs Law 1982, No. 7 of 1983. One thing to observe with this law is that it gave the chief executives of local government councils more powers than the emirs in the different emirates in the state. This is because they determined the composition of the Interpretation and Admonishing Committee. The ulama also were not given much of a role, and with the emirs their targets were the *gardawa* Muslim group. When the Maitatsine uprising occured, the need to strengthen the law became overwhelming.

1982 Religious Preaching Law

The Kano State law for the Establishment of the Council for Islamic Affairs, 1982 was designed also to regulate Islamic religious preaching specifically, in contrast to the old law which dealt with Qur'anic interpretation at the same time. It created the Kano State Council for Islamic Religious Affairs in all the local government areas of the state to complement the effort of the Interpretation and Admonishing Committees created under the 1970 law.

As part of the innovation in the the 1982 law, emirs and the ulama were given more powers by making the composition of the committee broader. New functions and powers were also provided. As regards their composition, seventeen people, all "learned in Islamic Religious Knowledge", representing various constituencies in the state: a chairman; three representatives of religious organisations from Kano City, one to represent the State Ministry of Education, one to represent the business interests, one from each area demarcated for the eight emirs in the state, one to represent the Council of Chiefs, one to represent the Department of Islamic Studies of Bayero University and other Higher Islamic Institutions, and a legal practitioner learned in both Islamic law and the common law. The Governor, rather than the head of any local government council, was given the power to appoint all the members of the committee and give them attendance and travelling allowances as he deems fit. Also, he gives the council directions of a general or specific character on the performance of any of the council's functions under the law. There was a new provision stating the specific aim of the law: to promote religious stability in the state and check religious activities, probably because of the Maitatsine challenge.

The functions of the council are to advise state and local governments on religious affairs and "on ways to check religious activities", public enlightenment on Islamic religious matters through publications and the mass media; radio, television, newspapers, magazines, journals and pamphlets and through seminars, workshops, public lectures and symposia, regulation of religious organisations by means of the issue of regulations, registration, the revocation of registrations in appropriate cases, the regulation of the admonishing and interpretation duty through the issue of permits to admonish or interpret and the revocation of permits as appropriate. Both the 1970 and 1982 laws continued as laws of the state until section 20 of Kano's Religious Preaching Law 1985 repealed both of them; rules on the control of Qur'anic interpretation and admonishing promulgated by the Kano Local Government Authority in 1970, and Kano State Law of 1982 Establishing a Council for Islamic Affairs for the State, which evidently had something to do with the regulation of preaching.

1985 Religious Law

The design of the Kano State Religious Preaching Law of 1985 was related to the measures taken by the military administration headed by Major General Muhammadu Buhari in 1983 in reaction to the two crises in Borno and Kaduna States; Bullum Kuttu between 26 and 29 November 1982 and Rigassa between 26^{h} and 30 October 1982 respectively. This two crises that involved the followers of Maitatsine, who died on 29 December 1980 in Kano during the Maitatsine crisis. It was stated in the preceding paragraphs that this military government also banned open-air religious preaching like its predecessor. But, in contrast, it did so in reaction to the Bullum Kuttu and Rigassa violent uprisings. One of the measures they took was to proscribe the Maitatsine movement on 8 November 1982. They also empowered the emirs in the affected states to control religious preaching in Friday mosques and religious preaching generally in their areas. This may be a possible explanation of why the 1985 law empowered the emirs to control preaching; Kano State may have decided to amend the law in conformity with the measures taken by the military regime.

Establishment and Nature

The 1985 law was designed to regulate Islamic religious preaching in Kano State. A combined reading of its establishment provisions in sections 1, 3(1) and 6(1) attests to this assertion. Section 1 of the law provides that "the law may be cited as the Religious Preaching Law". Sections 3(1) and 6(1) however clarify the Islamic nature of the law. It should be noted that this law establishes two types of committee. One is a committees for each emirate and one for each local government council. Section 3(1) provides that there shall be established for each emirate a committee to be known as the Committee for Islamic Religious Preaching, and section 6(1) makes provision for the establishment of subcommittees for Islamic religious preaching in each local government council in the state. These committees were given compositions, functions and tenure of office. One innovation in this regard is that the law gave more powers to the emirs and accommodated more experts on Islamic studies to participate in the operation of the committees in each emirate and in each local government council in the state, in contrast to the two previous 1970 and 1982 laws.

Emirate Committee for Islamic Religious Preaching

Composition

The composition of the Committee for Islamic Religious Preaching in the emirates is provided for under section 3(1)(2)(3)(4) and (5) of the law. The committee is made up of a chairman and no fewer than six other members who shall all be renowned Islamic religious scholars of high repute. The Chairman and the other members of the Committee shall be appointed by the Governor in consultation with the Emirate Council. The Secretary of the Emirate Council shall serve as the Secretary to the Committee. The Governor may in the public interest establish any other committee or committees in respect of any other religious organisation or denomination consisting mainly of its members to regulate preaching by such religious organisation or denomination.

Function

The functions of this committee are to receive applications for preaching permits, to examine and approve or disqualify an applicant for a preaching permit, to grant preaching permits to applicants, to establish and regulate standards for the examination and qualification of religious preachers, to open and keep a register of preachers and to enter the names and particulars of preachers in accordance with the provisions of this Law, to co-operate with all other committees of the state for the purpose of establishing a uniform standard and practice for the examination and qualification of preachers; and to do any other act or thing that may be necessary for carrying into effect the provisions of this Law.

Tenure and Removal

Subsection (4) provides for the members' tenure in office and their removal by the Governor. The committee members are to serve for three-year terms which are renewable once. They may resign on their own volition. Where they are unable to perform their functions or are guilty of misconduct the Governor may remove them.

Local Government Council Subcommittee for Islamic Religious Preaching

Composition

The local government council committee is established under section 6(1)(2)(3)and (4) of the law. Section 6(1) establishes in each local government council a subcommittee called the Subcommittee for Islamic Religious Preaching. The sub-committees differ in their composition and functions from the Committee for Islamic Religious Preaching in the emirates. A subcommittee shall be composed of the Chief Executive Officer of the Local Government Council who shall be Chairman; all the District Heads in the local government council;, the Divisional Police Officer in the local government council; the Chief Imam in the headquarters of the local government council; the Education Officer in charge of Islamic Education in the local government council; the Social Welfare Officer in charge of the local government council; and two other members who shall be Muslims of high repute and well versed in Islamic religious matters.

The law also provides that except in the case of ex officio members, the members of the subcommittee shall be appointed by the Commissioner for Local Government in consultation with the committee. Section 2 of the law defines the committee as the Committee for Islamic Religious Preaching established under section 3 and the commitees established in emirates. In addition, the secretary of the local government council shall serve as the secretary to the subcommittee in the area of authority of that local government council. In terms of their tenure in office and removal, subcommittee members are to hold office for three years and are eligible for reappointment. They may resign on their own volition. And where they are unable to perform their functions or are guilty of misconduct the Governor may remove them.

Function

In terms of their functions, section 8(1) of the law provides that the subcommittee shall be responsible for receiving applications from applicants for a preaching permit, forwarding such applications to the Committee to which it is responsible, monitoring the movement and activities of every holder of a preaching permit in the local government council area, keeping a register of all holders of preaching permits in the local government council area, causing the arrest of any person preaching without a permit or contrary to the conditions of his permit, and carrying out such other functions as may from time to time be directed by the Committee. Subsection (2) of this section however provides that each subcommittee shall be responsible and accountable to the committee under which it is established for the performance of its functions under this Law. This means that subcommittees are accountable to the emirate councils under which they are established.

Procedure and Allowances for Both Committees

Section 9 of the law provides that the committees and subcommittees are entitled to determine their own quorums and regulate their own procedure; further, that the validity of their proceedings is not affected by vacancies, defects in appointment, or the participation of persons not entitled to do so. Section 10 provides for their allowances: it states that the members of these committees may be paid such allowances as the Governor may approve.

Procedure for Grant and Punishment for Preaching without a Preaching Licence

Section 11 of the law makes provision for the procedure of application for a preaching permit, its revocation and punishment for contravening the law or conditions stipulated in the preaching permit. Subsection (1) provides that no person shall enage in religious preaching of any Islamic injunctions in any public place without a preaching permit. Section 18 of the law makes provision for punishment for preaching without a licence or in contravention of its conditions. Subsection (1) also provides that any preacher who preaches without a valid permit or preaches contrary to any conditions or order imposed pursuant to this Law, or publicly insults or seeks to excite contempt of any religious denomination in such manner as may be likely to lead to disorder or a breach of the peace commits an offence. Subsection (2) provides that the punishment is imprisonment for a term of not less than three years for a first offence; for a second or subsequent offence with imprisonment for a term of not less than five years and a fine of ten thousand naira.

Subsection (2) of section 11 provides that any person may apply for a permit to preach Islamic religious injunctions by submitting an application in writing to a subcommittee through the district head of his area. The application shall be accompanied by such information and particulars as the committee may prescribe. On receipt of the application, the subcommittee shall forward it to the appropriate committee (the emirate committee) for action. Section 12 sets out the kind of action to be taken on receipt of an application for a preaching permit and the conditions under which it can be granted or rejected. The section provides that the committee may grant the application if it is satisfied that the applicant has the requisite knowledge and experience to be a preacher of Islamic religious injunctions, that he is a Muslim scholar of high repute and is capable of complying with the conditions attached to the preaching permit. In order to convince itself of the applicant's qualifications, subsection (2) of this section allows the committee to examine the applicant orally, in writing or in such other manner as the committee may consider fit. Subsection (3) provides that where the committee is satisfied that an applicant is not qualified to preach it shall refuse the application.

Section 13 concerns the issue of the preaching permit or licence. Subsection (1) provides that the committee shall issue to every person whose application is granted under section 12 a preaching permit which shall entitle the applicant to preach in the local government area to which it relates or any of its parts as the permit may specify. Subsection (2) provides that where the committee considers it necessary, it may state on the permit such conditions or restrictions to which the holder shall be subject, including limiting him to preaching on a particular subject or period, restricting him to preach only in a particular town, village or specified number of towns or villages, and any other condition the committee may deem it fit to impose. Subsection (4) of the Law states that a preaching permit granted under this Law shall be signed by the secretary to the appropriate committee and is not transferable to any other person. It is renewable at the expiration of the period prescribed in the permit.

Revocation of a Preaching Permit

Section 14 concerns the way in which the preaching is conducted. It states that all preaching shall be conducted in a calm and orderly manner without the advocation of acrimony or abuse. Section 15 provides that a police officer or member of a subcommittee may order the holder of any preaching permit granted under this Law to produce it for inspection, and the holder shall comply with such order. Section 16 concerns revocation of the preaching permit. It provides that a Committee may revoke a preaching permit if it is satisfied that the preacher has violated the conditions attached to the preaching permit or any provisions of this Law, or the preacher has obtained the preaching permit by fraudulent means, or it is in the public interest to do so.

Borno

Like the regulation of religious preaching in Kano State, the case of Borno was also a collaboration between the authorities and dominant sufi religious groups/orders to repress the minority religious groups. The Borno experience also indicates that competition for space between main-line and minority religious groups led to the persecution of the latter group, always with the support of the state the ultimate aim of which was to neutralise their competitiveness. Ultimately, their suppression may have contributed to the crises in the state. For example, the Boko Haram imbroglio started in Borno State and later blossomed into an insurgency that threatened Nigeria and the west African sub-region at large. It continued with shootings and indiscriminate bombings until the Mohammadu Buhari administration introduced new strategies to confront it. It should be noted that Borno State, like Kano, had its own Islamic Religious Preaching Board Law in operation when the Boko Haram's embarrassing situation started in the state.

It is however pertinent to mention that Borno State was the second state to enact an Islamic Religious Preaching Board Law in Northern Nigeria in 1977. This law was enacted because of the activities of the *gardawa* religious group in Maiduguri which manifested itself in their religious preaching sessions at *Kukar 'Yan Bori* in Gwange ward in early 1970.[88] Between 1977 and 1979 in Maiduguri, this religious group enagaged in constant religious propaganda in which it attacked flamboyance and affluence in people's lives. Due to their pattern of religious preaching, their beliefs and religious practices such as their pattern of interpretation of the Qur'an, timing and structure of salat (prayer) and, significantly, their opinion on the books of Hadith and other sources of Shari'ah besides the Qur'an, they were always at loggerheads with other Muslims.[89] It was this experience in Borno and the experience in Kano that gave rise to the enactment of the religious preaching law in Borno State in 1977,[90] making the state the second state in Northern Nigeria to enact such a law. A possible explanation for this is that many *gardawa* who suffered suppression in Kano between 1973 and 1975 relocated to Maiduguri in Borno State to reside in Gwange ward.[91] This include those who were released from detention in 1975, as mentioned elsewhere in this work. They later relocated to Bullum Kuttu because of their awful relationship with people in Gwange ward.[92] The situation became tense in 1981, especially with the return of more *gardawa* to this area after Maitatsine's downfall in 1980. The state responded by amending and replacing the Religious Preaching Board Law of 1977 with the Islamic Preaching Board law of 1981.

The situation remained calm until sometime in July 1982 when the Borno State Intelligence Committee reported to the Commissioner of Police of the state on the group's new strategy which saw it reorganising its followers in large numbers in Bullum Kuttu and in other towns such as Biu, Gujba and

---

88 Auwal, A., *Gardawa, Ulama and the State in Northern Nigeria: The Maitatsine Phenomenon, 1962–1985* (Ph.D diss., unpublished, University of Maiduguri, 1998) at p. 157.

89 Ibid.

90 Ibid.

91 Ibid., pp. 158–160.

92 Ibid.

Gashua in the state.[93] The Commissioner of Police of Borno State in the person of Tahir Jidda again received another security report on 19 October 1982 on the activities of followers of Maitatsine in the same Bullum Kuttu who had allegedly planned to eliminate some people in the state. Based on these security reports, the security agencies arrested sixteen of them at their preaching session near the Shehu of Borno's palace on 25 October 1982. The next day, 26 October 1982, the police convened a meeting with members of the Islamic Religious Preaching Board in the state at the end of which the police advised the Preaching Board under the leadership of Shaikh Sherif Ibrahim Saleh to design control measures to stop unorthodox Islamic religious preaching in the state.[94] A question to ask here is what constitutes unorthodox religious preaching? How is it determined and who is competent to determine it?

The whole situation ended in a collision between the *gardawa* and the police which later became known as the Bullum Kuttu crisis in Borno State. The police succeeded in overpowering the group and in the process killed the leader of the group in the person of Muhammadu Rufa'i (alias Gajere).[95] In addition, a total of one hundred and eighteen people including sixteen police officers lost their lives in the encounter. A commission of inquiry into the unrest was later set up and one of its findings was that there was a direct link between the *gardawa* in Bullum Kuttu and the Maitatsine in Kano which made them his true followers.[96] This was the situation up to 2009 when the Boko Haram insurgency broke out in Borno State, as a result of which the 1981 religious preaching law was amended and replaced with the Borno State Islamic Preaching Board Law 2010.

Analysis of Religious Preaching Laws in Borno 1977–1981

As stated in the preceding paragraphs, Borno State was the second state to enact a religious preaching law in reaction to religious preaching associated with an Islamic religious group in the state. The law is entitled the "Admonishing and Interpretation Law, 1977." It was promulgated, like that of Kano, as an edict of the then Military Governor of the state, and it took effect on 1 August 1977. It regulates religious preaching generally in Borno State. Its section 2 deals with the interpretation of terms. Two terms were given meanings: an "admonisher" is a person who preaches with or without reading from any written document which contains any religious instructions, and "interpretation" was defined as

93 Ibid., p. 157.

94 Ibid., p. 162.

95 Ibid., p. 164.

96 Ibid., p. 166.

'any person taking part or contributing to any interpretation'. The law here appears to be regulating religious preaching in a general sense. Sections 3 and 4 of the the law provide for punishments. Section 3 punishes any admonisher or any interpreter who interprets any religious text either orally or in written form in any language without a licence and utters wounding statements.

Section 5 empowers the Governor to establish admonishing and interpretation committees for each local government area in the state. This committee shall be responsible for the issue of permits to intending religious preachers on certain conditions, and such permits must be signed by the secretary of the local government council before they become valid. In addition, the law confers power on the committees to revoke permits where such is recommnended in any criminal proceedings against the holder of a permit. Also the committees are given powers to exercise their discretion with regard to renewal of the permit, refusal to issue or renew it for preachers and prescribing conditions, and they are entitled not to give any reason for refusing to issue a permit, renew it or even revoke it. It is noteworthy however that the law did not provide any guidance on how the committees are to exercise these powers.

Section 6(1) empowers some persons to inspect preaching permits at any time. It provides that any member of a local government police committee, any member of the admonishing and interpretation committee, the secretary to the local government, and a district or village head of the area has the right to require holders of a preaching permit to produce it for inspection at any time. Refusal to produce it on demand constitutes an offence under the law and the offender is liable on conviction to a fine not exceeding two hundred naira or to imprisonment not exceeding one month, or both.

Section 7 of the law, however, exempts from punishment any admonishing or interpretation to students in any place for the purpose of learning or over the radio or on the television in an organised programme for the general enlightenment of members of the public. What comes within the purview of general "enlightenment" is not defined by the law. This may create a problem.

Section 8 provides that where there is no prescribed penalty, the person shall be liable on conviction to a fine not exceeding five hundred naira or imprisonment not exceeding six months or both. This law operated until it was repealed by section 23 of the Islamic Religious Preachings Law, 1981 "in so far as it applies to Islamic Religious Preachings."

1981–2010

This was the second religious preaching law in Borno State. The provisions of this law show a complete shift from the regulation of religious preaching in general to the regulation of a specific religion—Islamic Religious Preaching.

This may not be unconnected with the fact that problems experienced in the state are associated with Islamic religious groups and no others. This is reflected in the provisions of the law. For example, its enactment clause in section 1 provides that the law may be cited as the Islamic Religious Preaching Law, 1981[97] and it came into operation on 23 June 1981. Its section 2 sets out the meaning of some terms as applied in the law which further reveals the Islamic nature of the law. The meaning of the terms indicates specificifically that the law was designed to regulate the religion of Islam only. For example, section 2 defines "Board" to mean the Islamic Religious Preaching Board established under section 3 of the law. It defines "Committee" as the Islamic Religious Preaching Advisory Committee established under section 7 of the law and "Preacher" as a person who preaches with or without a document which contains any Islamic Religious Instructions. The imam of *sallatul-idein* was also given the meaning of a person who leads congregational prayer during Muslim festival prayers and so on.

Section 3 of the law establishes the state body called the Islamic Religious Preaching Board and its composition. From the content of the provisions, the law gives the Governor a lot of powers in the formation of the Board. This calls the independence of the Board into question. The Board comprises a chairman to be appointed by the Governor; one representative from each emirate council, to be so appointed by the council; three other representatives from among Islamic religious preachers in the state, to be appointed by the Governor; and three other persons to be appointed by the Governor. The Governor again shall appoint the secretary of the Board. The law does not make any provision on how the Governor determines his choice of appointments and what factors to consider in doing so.

A key person in Borno State provided general information in an interview on why the Borno state Islamic religious preaching board law was enacted and how it operates. According to Sheikh Goni Mohammed Saad Ngamdu[98] the enactment of the Islamic Preaching Board law in 1981 was aimed at controlling Islamic religious preachers who engage in Islamic religious preaching without "proper knowledge, preaching just anyhow; especially Izala coming to criticize and make trouble in the state."

---

97 See Borno State of Nigeria Gazette No. 14, Vol. 3 15 December 1981.

98 He is the North East Zonal Coordinator Jama'atu Nasril Islam and Borno State Secretary General of the same organisation. He gave this information on 12 May 2012 in an interview he granted with Dr. Philip Ostien; formerly of the Faculty of Law of the University of Jos in Nigeria, a copy of which is with the author.

According to him, the board comprises a Chairman, one representative from each emirate council, to be appointed by the council and three representatives from the group of Islamic religious preachers in the state. The Governor nominated Sheikh Goni Mohammed Saad Ngamdu of the Jama'atul Nasril Islam who is a known member of the Tijjaniyya group, Sheikh Muhammad Abba Aji, a known Wahabi/Izala member and Goni Sanda, a neutral party. The Governor also nominated three other people, Sheikh Ibrahim Salih, Sheikh Abubakar el-Miskin, a popular Tijaniya adherent, and Goni Kaltumi, a popular adherent of Tijjaniyya sufi group.[99] These "preachers" and "other persons" remained on the board until 2010 but before the amendment of the law.[100]

In terms of functions, the Board was to determine and regulate the qualifications required of any person to become an Islamic religious preacher or a Qur'anic interpreter and make recommendations to the appropriate emirate council, to conduct examinations and set standards for any person desirous of becoming an Islamic religious preacher or a Qur'anic interpreter, to compile and approve sets of Islamic religious poetry or songs that may be permitted in mosques or in public places and to regulate and determine the type of Islamic religious poetry or sogns to be approved for public consumption and dissemination in public preachings or places of worship.

According to the interviewee, the committee had issued preaching licences to intending Islaimc religious preachers on specific subjects in the state. They did not discriminate on the basis of sect in their operations. They only tried to be sure that a preacher knew whatever subject it was that he wanted to preach. Nevertheless, in some instances there were complaints: people who were disqualified or unqualified and not given licences would say that they had been discriminated against because of their beliefs. There are also instances where the Board even withdrew the licences (or certificates) of some preachers. For example, at some point the Board withdrew the preaching licence of Sheikh Muhammad Abba Aji because he was causing "confusion," calling other Muslims unbelievers. Another example was one Usman Bida; he was asked to give his opinion on the relationship between Muslims and non-Muslims. He said: "War!" His licence was suspended for two years. But the Islamic Preaching Board Law still exists in Borno State and it issued about 500 licences between 1981 and 2010 when an amendment of the law was effected.[101]

---

99 Their affiliation to the Tijaniya sufi order is well known in Nigeria.

100 Referring to when the interview was granted.

101 As at 2012.

Sheikh Ngandu, continuing his comments, stated further that despite the law being in operation, many people had preached without a licence over the years and had not been prosecuted. On Boko Haram he said that they had prepared and submitted to the government reports on people preaching without licences generally in the state and those preaching hatred on the "religious unbelief" of others, and Muhammad Yusuf was one of those people. Nothing however came out of their report. Why was it impossible for the government to apply the preaching law effectively in the state long before the unfortunate event? Also according to Kadi Abubakar Imam,[102] Mohammed Yusuf had been on the board of the Borno State Sharia Implementation Committee from 2003 and had been collecting his allowances up to the time when he was extra-judicially killed. He was also on religious committees in Yobe State and had been collecting salaries from government while at the same time preaching to people that it was Haram to do so. It may however be argued that he may have been influenced by the Sharia posture of the agencies since anything that agrees with Sharia could be acceptable to him.[103]

The 1981 law also established local government committees in each local government area of the state. Section 6 establishes the Islamic Religious Preaching Advisory Committee in each local government area of the state. Section 7 makes provision for the committee's composition. The committee consist of the following as members: the secretary to the local government council, all Distict Heads within the local government area, two respectable Islamic religious preachers from each District, two people to be nominated by the local government council, a learned and respectable Islamic religious leader in the area to be the Chairman. Subsection (2) of section 6 mandates the Governor to appoint the committee for each local government area.

The functions of the local government committees are to receive and forward applications to the Board with two recent passport photographs from persons of no less than 25 years old intending to be Islamic religious preachers or Qur'anic interpreters; to advise the Board on matters referred to in section 5 of the law generally; and such other matters as the Board may from time to time determine. Sections 9 and 10 provide for the quorum for the Board's meetings—one-third of the total number of the members at the date of the

102 He was a Kadi at the Sharia Court of Appeal, Maiduguri, and the secretary of the management committee of the Al-Amin Daggash Mosque where Yusuf used to preach once a week. He gave the information when he granted an interview with Ostien also on 12 May 2012, a copy of which is with the author.

103 Ibid.

meeting and so on—and the power of each of the committees to regulate their own procedure respectively.

Section 11 allows each emirate council to issue licences to persons found to be fit and proper to preach on the recommendation of the Board. Section 13 however provides that where it appears to the Board that any person recommended by the Board to be an Islamic religious preacher is for any reason unable or unsutable to continue as such, it may at any time recommend to the appropriate emirate council the withdrawal of of his licence. Subsection (2) allows the emirate council under section 1 above to revoke the licence and give notice in writing of the revocation of the licence to the person concerned and the secretary of the local government area. Sub-section (3) provides that the recommendation of the Board on the issue of renewal, refusal to issue or renew or revocation of any licence and addition to, alteration or cancellation of any prescribed conditions shall be at the discretion of the Board which, before taking a decision, shall provide an opportunity for the person whose rights and obligations may be affected to make representations to it. Subsection (4) provides that a preaching licence under this law shall be revoked where in any criminal proceedings, however arising, any court recommends to the Board that the licence be revoked.

Section 14 criminalises any Islamic religious preaching in a public place, including a mosque, without a preaching licence. Subsection (2) provides for the manner in which religious preaching should be conducted, basically that it should be conducted in a calm and orderly manner.

Section 18 provides for circumstances under which a preacher may be said to have breached the law. The section provides that a person who preaches without a licence or permit or, where licensed to preach, he preaches in contravention of the conditions of the licence or, when asked to stop preaching by the appropriate authority, he refuses to stop, or uses unapproved poetry or songs in Islamic religious preaching, or by any means publicly insults or seeks to incite contempt for any Islamic religious sect in such manner as to be likely to lead to a breach of the peace, or interprets any Islamic religious text either orally or in writing in any language without licence. The section provides that where there is no prescribed penalty, the person shall be liable on conviction to a fine not exceeding two hundred naira or imprisonment not exceeding six months or both. Section 20 empowers the Area Court or other courts of equivalent jurisdiction to try offences committed under this law, but exempts the Imam of a Friday mosque congregation or Imam of *sallatul-idein* congregational prayer from the application of the law. The situation remained like this until 2010 when the Boko Haram conflict began in earnest in Borno

State. In reaction, among other measures the state amended and replaced the 1981 Islamic Religious Preaching Law with the Islamic Religious Preaching Law 2010.

The 2010 Islamic Religious Preaching Law of Borno State

The situation under which this was enacted need not be repeated here. The Law, like that of Kano, is designed to regulate Islamic preaching only. Its section 1 provides that it may be cited as the "Borno State Islamic Religious Preaching Law 2010" and it came into operation on 30 July 2010. It is almost the same as the 1981 law but differs only in the composition and some aspect of the functions of the Board. In terms of composition, the number of persons to be nominated was increased even as the Governor still retains his powers of appointment. The Board consists of a chairman who is to be appointed by the Governor, one representative from each emirate council, six representatives of *ulama* to be recommended by the emirate councils and approved by the Governor, six other persons to be appointed by the Governor on their personal merit, a representative of the Ministry responsible for religious affairs not below the rank of Director, and a representative each from all the registered Islamic Organisations. The Board shall be responsible for determining, regulating and screening of persons intending to be preachers. By recognising only registered Islamic organisations, the new Law was able to exclude organisations such as Boko Haram from membership of the Board.

In terms of functions, section 5 of the Law stipulates that the board shall determine and regulate the qualifications required for any person to become an Islamic preacher or a Qur'anic interpreter and submit recommendations to the appropriate emirate council of satisfactory applications received by them, to conduct examinations and set standards for any person desirous of becoming an Islamic religious or Qur'anic interpreter, to compile and approve sets of Islamic religious poetry, songs or literature that may be permitted in mosques or in public places, to regulate and determine the type of Islamic religious poetry, songs or literature to be approved for public consumption and dissemination in public preaching or places of worship, to carry out any other function that may be referred to it by the Council of *ulama* in the state or by the state government.

Kaduna State

A lot was said already about what happened between Kano and Kaduna in the earlier sections on the control of religious preaching in Northern Nigeria. Kaduna State, being the old capital of the northern region, experienced a lot of religious activity during the time of late Sardauna of Sokoto. Therefore it suffices to start by saying that Kaduna State, like Kano and Borno, experienced its own version of mutiny associated with Islamic religious groups: Maitatsine and Shiite separatism are examples. It was as a result of these two experiences that the state enacted its first religious preaching law called the Kaduna State Religious Preaching Edict No. 7 of 1984. This law remained in operation up to 1987 when it was amended by the Regulation of Religious Preaching Amendment Edict No. 1 of 1987, and later by the Preaching Law No. 6 of 1996. The 1996 law continued to be in operation until December 2015 when the state experienced the Shiite clash with the convoy of the Chief of Army Staff of the Nigerian Army, as a result of which the state proposed to repeal and replace the 1996 preaching law in the state with the Kaduna State Religious Preaching Bill, 2016, which is currently being passionately debated in the state and Nigeria at large.

As far as Kaduna State is concerned, its first negative religious upheaval was the offshoot of the Maitasine unrest that happened in Kano. It happened in Rigassa in Kaduna State between 29 and 30 October 1982. Although it was not as devastating as those of Kano and Borno States, it is however important to talk about it because of its coincidence with the Bullum Kuttu turbulence in Borno State. According to Anwar, the resurgence of the *gardawa* with new vigour in defence of their right to freedom of religion almost exactly two years after the downfall of Maitatsine says a lot about their cleverness, which contradicts people's belief that the group was a group of badly informed and disordered people.[104]

The sufi brotherhoods in Kaduna State firmly believed that Kaduna had been a home for the *gardawa* religious preachers because of the sense of accommodation given to them by Sheikh Gumi even though he denied this allegation, as discussed elsewhere in this work.[105] But security reports from the police however reveal that the *gardawa* had been residing in Rigassa, Kaduna State, since 1981.[106] The fact of the matter is that on 25 October 1982 the Commissioner of Police of Kaduna State received a report indicating the influx and regrouping of *gardawa* religious preachers in Rigassa in Kaduna State. In order to ascertain their aim, the Commissioner of Police authorised one Karimu Yakubu; an Acting Assistant Commissioner of Police in charge of Kaduna metropolis, to verify the information through people like the Village Head of Rigassa, the

104 Anwar, A., *Gardawa, ulama and the State of Northern Nigeria: The Maitatsine phenomenon, 1962–1985* (Ph.D diss., University of Maiduguri, 1998), p. 4.

105 Ibid., p. 168.

106 Ibid.

District Head of Rigachikun and some known ulama in the state in order to take corrective measures.[107]

On 29 October 1982 the officer in company with some other officers moved straight to Rigassa where they arrested about fifty *gardawa*. However, the arrested people could not be moved to the police station because other *gardawa* came out in large numbers and engaged the police in a real fight. The *gardawa* attacked the police with weapons including poisoned arrows and so on,[108] whereby several police officers were killed. The riot subsequently spread into the town of Kaduna where the rioters attacked and killed innocent people.[109] The police later brought the situation under control.

The second significant religious incident in Kaduna State was the crisis associated with the shi'ite group otherwise called the Islamic Movement of Nigeria. This Islamic religious group emerged on the Nigerian scene as the insidious effect of a combination of three things; the expulsion of Ibrahim Yaqoub al-Zakzaky from Ahmadu Bello University, Zaria; the influx of Islamic books from countries such as Egypt,[110] Iran, Saudi Arabia and Turkey into Nigeria; and their accessability to Ahmadu Bello University (ABU) students, particularly after the Iranian revolution of 1979.[111]

The shi'ites began as a group in Nigeria in the early 1980s with Ibrahim Yaqoub al-Zakzaky as their leader. Al-Zazaky was a product of the Muslim Student Society of Nigeria (MSSN),[112] and his name came into the public domain when the management of Ahmadu Bello University, Zaria, expelled him from the university as a result of the key role he played in the popular "Islam Only" demonstration organised by the Muslim Student Society of Nigeria (MSSN) in 1977, in which the group called for the adoption of an Islamic government in Nigeria.[113] His expulsion from the university paved the way for his invitation to visit Iran where he explored shi'ite doctrines.[114] It should be noted that before his expulsion from Ahmadu Bello University, Zaria, Zakzaky had already become radicalised and exposed to shi'ite doctrine as a result of contacts with different Islamic writings coming into the country from radical

107 Ibid., p. 169.

108 Ibid.

109 Ibid., p. 170.

110 See Hassan, I.H., "An Introduction to Islamic Movements and Modes of Thought in Nigeria", in Denzer, L., and Shereikis, R. (eds), *PAS/ISITA Working Papers No. 1*. Evanston, IL: Program of African Studies, North-western University, 2015, pp. 24–26.

111 Ibid.

112 Ibid.

113 Ibid.

114 Ibid.

groups in Egypt, Iran and Turkey.[115] It was this scenario that provided the fertile ground for the emergence of the shi'ite movement in Nigeria.

The main obsession of the group has always been protesting against what it termed the anti-Islamic posture of the Nigerian government, and at various times they called for the establishment in Nigeria of a government similar to that of Iran.[116] To achieve their aims, they adopted the well-known shi'ite methodology of Taqiyya, or disguise of religious conviction.[117] They maintain a strong opposition to secularism and seek to establish an Islamic government in Nigeria headed by their fellow shi'ite members. In addition, in their public religious preaching sessions they insult, denigrate and attack the persons of the first three Caliphs—Abu-Bakr, Umar and Usman—as being usurpers of the succession to Prophet Muhammad which they believe rightfully belonged to Ali, and also legitimise Mut'a marriage, a form of temporary marriage considered unlawful by sunni Muslims. These are classical shi'ite doctrines. The sunni Muslims that constitute the majority in Nigeria despise the shi'ite for these allegations and disrespect. Their belief, however, is that the time to take up arms is not ripe in Nigeria and nobody knows when the time will be ripe enough for them to take up revolutionary arms to change the government, as occurred in Iran.

The adoption of the Taqiyya methodology has created fear in the minds of other Nigerian Muslims on the one hand, and of the Nigerian government on the other. This is a possible explanation of why the shi'ite are always under strong suspicion from government and the people. It may also be true to say that it is this suspicion that triggers conflict between the group and government security outfits at various times.[118] For example, during its silver jubilee celebrations on 10 April 2005, the movement affirmed its ultimate aim to establish an Islamic government in Nigeria, but this brought it into conflict with the government.[119] It also clashed with Nigerian security outfits at several

115 Ibid.

116 Ibid.

117 Ibid.

118 Ibid.

119 See the official website of the Islamic Movement of Nigeria (IMN), http://islamicmovement.org, with a Hausa version at http://www.harkarmusulunci.org, and an Arabic version at http://www.alharka.net, for more information on their activities. The websites discuss such important shia ideas and rituals as Ashura, the birthday of Zahra (*Maulud*), *idul Ghadir*, and others. Furthermore, the discourses of Imam Ruhollah Moosavi Khomeini, Imam Ali Hosseini Khamenei and other shi'a scholars are presented on the websites, as well as shi'ite perspectives of sunni Islam, radicalism, terrorism, nationalism and

times resulting in the destruction of the group's headquarters in Sokoto in July 2007 and in Zaria in 2009 and 2014.[120]

Its latest clash with the security forces in Nigeria was on 12 December 2015 in the city of Zaria in Kaduna State. The members of the Islamic Movement of Nigeria were conducting their usual *tattaki* (a religious procession) in the city of Zaria, with thousands of their members out on the major streets of Zaria City. This blocked public roads and made it difficult for other road users to use the roads. Coincidentally, the Nigerian Chief of the Army Staff was on his way to visit the Emir of Zazzau, and he was forced to stop on the road because members of the shi'ite group blocked the way and refused the army Chief access despite entreaties from the army officers. Apparently, fearing for the safety of the army Chief, his security detail opened fire on the shi'ite procession, as a result of which many people died, and the shi'ite headquarters at Gyellasu in Zaria City, a complex building called "Hussainiya Bakiyatullah" serving as the group's headquarters and centre of their activities, was destroyed by the Nigerian army.

In reaction, the Kaduna State government introduced social control measures to control shi'ites in the state. First, the state proscribed all forms of road blocading, obstruction of public highways, and occupation of public facilities in a manner that disturbs other people in the state. It further directed people to apply for and obtain permission before they engaged in any form of procession in the state. Second, the state established a Commission of Inquiry to investigate the remote and immediate causes of the conflict between the Nigeria army and shi'ite members. Third, the state introduced a proposed law entitled "A bill for a law to substitute the Kaduna State Regulation of Religious Preaching", with a view to controlling religious preaching in the state.[121] As a final blow, the state banned and declared the Islamic movement of Nigeria an unlawful body in the state on the basis of the report of the Commission of Inquiry it set up to investigate the confrontation between the Nigerian army and the shi'ites.

Analysis of Religious Preaching Laws in Kaduna State

At the time of writing this paper, the government of Kaduna State had introduced a bill called the Religious Preaching Bill, 2016, seeking to substitute the

---

secularism. The websites also post material from the English-language *Pointer Express* and the Hausa *Mizan*)news magazines of the Zakzaky group.

120 Ibid.

121 "A Bill for a Law to Substitute the Kaduna State Regulation of Religious Preaching" (Amendment) Edict No. 6 of 1996.

state's Regulation of Religious Preaching (Amendment) Edicts No. 1 of 1987 and No. 6 of 1996. This proposed law was part of the reaction of the Kaduna State government to control the shi'ite -Army confrontation and other similar problems in the state.

Definition of a Religious Preacher

Section 3 of the proposed law defines a religious preacher as any person licensed by the Jama'atu Nasril Islam (JNI) or the Christian Association of Nigeria (CAN) to preach in the state. The JNI is a body established by the late Premier of Northern Nigeria in the 1960s to serve as an umbrella body for all Muslims in Northern Nigeria. It has branch offices in all the states of Northern Nigeria headed by emirs or persons appointed by them. These emirs are members of the dominant sufi religious groups, either Qadriyya/Tijaniyya or Tariqa. They are also mostly sunni Muslims and do not recognise the shi'ites as Muslims. The JNI had played a prominent role in the regulation of Islamic religious preaching in Northern Nigeria in the 1960s and 1970s.

For example, in 1970, when the ulama in Kano State, which consisted of members of the dominant sufi orders, influenced the enactment of a law to regulate Islamic religious preaching in Kano State, the minority *gardawa* groups suffered.[122] They were denied a licence to preach in the areas under the jurisdiction of Kano State, but they moved to Kaduna State and obtained preaching licences from the JNI.[123]

Again, section 3 of the proposed law on religious preaching states that any person not licensed by the JNI or the CAN may not be recognised as a religious preacher in the state. In the case of Muslims, this requirement has favoured dominant religious groups which are mostly sunni and which do not recognise shi'ites as Muslims. This is an obvious example of state favouritism extended to the dominant sects through the proposed law.

Recognition of Islam and Christianity as Major Religions

Section 4 of the proposed Law recognises Islam and Christianity as the two major religions in the state, and it establishes three committees to regulate the two religions. The Law recognises the strength of Izala as an Islamic organisation in the region. In recognition of the status the group achieved in the region

122 Kano Local Government Authority (Control of Quranic Interpretation and Admonishing) Rules 1970. This became Kano Local Government Law No. 3, 1970.

123 Anwar, A., *Gardawa, ulama and the State of Northern Nigeria: The Maitatsine phenomenon, 1962–1985* (Ph.D. diss., University of Maiduguri, 1998), p. 4.

in the 1970s and 1980s, the proposed Law gave Izala equal representation with Tariqa at the Interfaith Ministerial Committee appointed by the governor. It did the same thing in terms of recognising the authority of CAN membership over other Christian groups. But there are questions about where minority groups within the broader categories of Islam and Christianity fall. Christian Jehovah's Witnesses and Muslim Shi'ite and Ahmadiyya are examples of these intra-religious minority groups. Section 4(2) of the preaching bill provides for the establishment of a ministerial committee to be composed of: (1) a chairman appointed by the governor, (2) a special adviser to the governor on internal security, (3) a senior adviser to the governor on interfaith matters, (4) a member from the JNI and CAN, (5) a representative of the Ministry of Justice and (6) one representative each from the Nigerian Police, Department of State Security Service, and the Civil Defence Corps. In addition, the JNI and CAN are to maintain a record of churches and mosques including data on all preachers. Minority religious groups are not in contemplation as having representation or a role on the committee.

JNI and CAN Power over the Issue of Preaching Licences

Section 5 of the preaching bill empowers the committees of the JNI and CAN to issue licences to preachers for a period not exceeding one year, as approved by the ministerial committee. Although these two bodies existed long before the Kaduna State government designed its preaching laws, they had no power in law to issue preaching licences in Nigeria. The JNI had done this in the past but it had no official power to do so under the law. However, the preaching laws in Kaduna State had never been enforced, so there was no real way to know whether minority religious groups would have been able to obtain preaching licences in the state under this system. It does, however, suffice to say that the proposed law, along with the previous ones, seems not to contemplate the shi'ites, Ahmadiyya and other minority religious groups as likely recipients of a preaching licence.

Local Government Area Screening Committees

Section 6(1) of the proposed Law establishes in each Local Government Area a committee to screen applications for licences and recommend the same to the ministerial committee. Section 6(2) provides for the composition of the committee as follows: (1) the chairman and co-chairman each representing one of the two major religions (one Muslim and the other Christian) to be appointed by the Governor on the recommendation of the chairman of the Local Government Council, (2) a representative of the police, (3) two Muslims with one each representing the Izala[124] and Tariqa[125] religious groups, and (4) two representatives of CAN. The shi'ites and other minority Islamic and Christian religious groups do not appear to be in contemplation here.

Compliance with the Proposed Law

Section 7 of the bill empowers the Local Government Area committees to ensure compliance with the terms of the licence so issued and register accredited preachers of all religious groups and organisations operating in the Local Government Area.

Regulation of Communication

The preaching bill also contains a number of provisions regulating communication by religious groups. Section 9 allows all cassettes, CDs, flash drives and any other communication gadgets from accredited preachers to be played inside one's house, azure (entrance porch), church, mosque or any other designated place of worship. Section 10 provides that any cassette containing a religious recording in which abusive language is used against any person or religious organisation or religious leaders past or present is prohibited in the state.

Punishment

The proposed Law has a section prescribing punishments for contravention of the Law. Section 12 provides that:

> A person shall be guilty of an offence who in contravention of this law; (a) preaches without a valid license; (b) plays religious cassette or uses a loudspeaker for religious purpose after 8 pm in a public place; (c) uses a loudspeaker for religious purpose other than in a mosque or church and the surrounding areas outside the stipulated prayer times; (d) uses a loudspeaker in vehicles plying the streets with religious recording; (e) abuses religious books; (f) incites disturbance of the public peace; (g) abuses or uses any derogatory term in describing any religion: or (h) carries weapons of any description whether concealed or not in places of worship or to any other place with a view to causing religious disturbance shall be guilty of an offence.

124 A sunni Muslim group.

125 A sufi Muslim group.

The legal implication of this section as it relates to the shi'ites and other religious groups in the state is that they may not be able to obtain preaching licences because they are not considered to be Muslims by the majority sunni groups who have control over the committees set up to enforce the proposed Law. In addition, section 13 provides, "A person who commits an offence under the provision of this law shall be liable on conviction to a term of imprisonment not exceeding two years or a fine of two hundred thousand naira or both; and shall have his licence revoked." Section 14 of the Law confers sharia and customary courts with jurisdiction to punish violators of the Law.

Effects of the Measures and the Proposed Preaching Bill

Under this heading the effect of the social control measures, which involve measures of social control introduced by the state in banning all forms of road blocades, the obstruction of public highways and the occupation of public facilities in a manner that causes inconvenience to other citizens in the state, would be discussed first. Second, discussion on the effect of the proposed preaching Law will follow. The measures may appear innocuous, and for the maintenance of peace and order in the state, especially under section 45 of the Nigerian Constitution, which allows the state to use its regulatory power to limit citizens' freedom of religion in the interest of defence, public safety, public order, public morality or public health or for the purpose of protecting the rights and freedoms of others.

However, it should be noted that in some respects there is not much difference between the 1996 and the present proposed Law seeking to substitute for it. However, a key difference is that the 1996 edict was enacted under military rule, while the present proposed law was enacted under a democratically elected government. When scrutinised in the context of democracy, measures such as the ones above may not qualify as reasonable measures in a democracy, for several reasons.

First, the first set of measures was not prescribed by law as required in a democracy. Second, they are vague in every way and lack procedures for religious groups to apply for permission to conduct religious activities, such as the procession or other religious gatherings that may interfere with public roads and buildings as contained in the first social control measures mentioned at the beginning of this paper. Third, the measures lack mechanisms for protecting religious groups from discrimination, especially when such groups apply to embark on their religious activities. Fourth, the measures did not define the phrase "obstruction of public high ways" or specify who would be competent to determine it.

Fifth, the proposed law provided no information as to what would amount to inconveniencing other citizens and how to determine it, or what mechanism the authorities would apply to balance the competing rights without burdening the right of the citizen or compromising the neutrality of the state. Sixth, there is no specification of the punishment for contravention of the Law. In the absence of a specified punishment, it is not constitutional to punish a citizen of Nigeria for an offence that is not written down in law under section 36(8) of the Nigerian Constitution. Finally, it is not clear what type of evidence would be required to prove contravention of these measures in a court of law and by what means. This is especially important, because research into matters of this nature indicates that the process of the exercise of discretion in different legal orders is found to be susceptible to bias, especially where it involves groups whose ideologies disagree with predominant ideologies of majority groups in the state, as in the case of the shiites in both Kaduna State and Nigeria as a whole, where sunni Muslims are the dominant group.[126]

Ban and Declaration against the Islamic Movement in Nigeria

The Kaduna State government responded to the face-off between shia groups and the Nigerian army by introducing social control measures which have been discussed above, the introduction of the Religious Preaching Bill, 2016 to replace the state's Regulation of Religious Preaching (Amendment) Edicts No. 1 of 1987 and No. 6 of 1996. The final crackdown on the shi'ite group known as the Islamic Movement of Nigeria came on 7 October 2016, when the Kaduna State government issued an order entitled the Kaduna State Gazette No. 21 of 7 October 2016 which banned and declared the Islamic Movement in Nigeria an unlawful society in Kaduna State.[127]

The Kaduna State Government relied on section 45(1) of the Constitution of Nigeria, which gives the state its regulatory power to restrict citizens' freedom of religion in the interest of defence, public safety, public order, public morality or public health or for the purpose of protecting the rights and freedoms of others, and section 97(A) of the Penal Code Law, Cap 110 Laws of Kaduna State 1991, which gives the Governor the power to declare as an unlawful society any organisation the activities of which are dangerous to the security and good governance of the state. To justify the declaration, the government based its decision on the finding of the judicial Commission of Inquiry it had set

126 See Richardson, J.T., (ed.), *Regulating Religion: Case Studies from Around the Globe* New York: Kluwer Academic/Plenum Publishers (2004), pp. 1–15.

127 See: 2016. *Kaduna State Official Gazette* No. 21, 7 October.

up. According to the government, the Commission of Inquiry found that the Islamic Movement in Nigeria is not a registered organisation; has a paramilitary wing and its members do not respect the laws of the country and duly constituted authorities; has overtly continued with unlawful procession, obstruction of facilities including schools without regard to the rights of other citizens and the public peace and order of the state. The Governor further stated that the group's actions, if allowed to go unchecked, will constitute a danger to the peace, tranquility, harmonious coexistence and governance of Kaduna State.[128]

It should be noted, however, that two days after the issue of this declaration, the governors of Kano, Plateau, Katsina and other states in Northern Nigeria issued similar declarations against the shi'ites in their states. These declarations came with devastating consequences for the members of the shi'a. This is because many people, including members of dominant religious groups in Kaduna, Plateau, Kano and many other states in Northern Nigeria took the law into their own hands and attacked members of the shia group in various states. As a result of this violence, many were killed and their property wantonly destroyed.[129]

Constitutional and Human Rights Discourse

Section 38(1) of the Constitution of the Federal Republic of Nigeria 1999 (as amended) makes provision for citizens' "freedom of thought, conscience and religion, including freedom to change his religion or belief, and freedom (either alone or in community with others, and in public or private) to manifest and propagate his religion or belief in worship, teaching, practice and observance." Section 39(1) further provides that "every person shall be entitled to freedom of expression, including freedom to hold opinions and to receive and impart ideas and information without interference," and section 40 provides that "every person shall be entitled to assemble freely and associate with other persons ..." these are the granting clauses that give a citizen of Nigeria the constitutional right to engage in religious propagation within the shores of Nigeria among other rights; to associate and to hold on to an opinion; or to impart ideas without any hindrance.

But these rights are not absolute. The Constitution gives the state power to derogate from them through laws that "are reasonably justifiable in a democratic society." This is called the derogation or limitation clause, and it is the basis of the state's regulatory power from which the state drives its power to

128 Kaduna State Official Gazette No. 21.

129 Ibid.

enact these Preaching Board Laws. Section 45(1) of the Constitution provides that "nothing shall invalidate any law that is reasonably justifiable in a democratic society in the interest of defence, public safety, public order, public morality or public health; or for the purpose of protecting the rights and freedoms of other persons." This leaves plenty of room for the more or less standard array of penal and other legislation which the state uses to restrict citizens' enjoyment of these rights. The questions are to what extent the state can restrict the enjoyment of these rights in a democratic society without necessarily violating the citizen's rights. Second, what would be the criteria or the judicial review mechanism to be employed and why? And how would that conform or conflict with free exercise of the substantive rights? This requires the courts in Nigeria to engage in the judicial review process. Unfortunately, courts in Nigeria are yet to get an adequate opportunity to make any pronouncement on the constitutionality or otherwise of any or all of the provisions of Preaching Board Laws.

Judicial Review of the Exercise of Freedom of Religion in Nigeria

There are two models of judicial review to be considered in this paper: the "American Model" and "the Continental European Model."[130] The American model is decentralised while the European Continental Model is centralised.[131] There is also a crossbreed of the two.[132] A particular legal order may provide for stronger or weaker judicial review.[133] But an important issue on judicial review is the method of interpretation employed by the courts in construing constitutional provisions.[134] In some legal systems, the parliament or the legislature is more powerful than the courts, such that any decision that did not go down well with them can be overturned.[135] This has implications for the role of the courts in filling normative gaps in the Constitution.

In Nigeria, the trend is that the courts will generally invalidate an enactment where it contravenes the procedure laid down in the Constitution as in *Attorney-General of Bendel State* v. *Attorney-General of the Federation and Ors*[136] or where the legislature is found to have exceeded its powers in the making of

---

130 See Chen, A.H.Y., and Maduro, M.P., "The Judiciary and Constitutional Review," in Tushnet, M., Fleiner, T., and Sauders, C. (eds), *Routledge Handbook of Constitutional Law* (Routledge, New York, 2013), pp. 97–107.

131 Ibid., pp. 98–97.

132 Ibid.

133 Ibid., pp. 97–105.

134 Ibid.

135 Ibid., pp. 104–105.

136 See (1982) 3 NCLR 358.

a law, as in *Lakanmi* v. *Attorney-General* (*Western Region*) *and Ors*[137] or where legislation contravenes the provisions of the Fundamental Human Rights Chapter of the Constitution, as in *Shugaba Darman* v. *Minister of Internal Affairs and Ors*,[138] or where the exercise of powers of one organ usurps the constitutional powers of the other organ or otherwise contravenes the provisions of the Constitution, as in *Attorney-General of Ogun State* v. *Attorney-General of the Federation and Ors*[139] and finally where any legislation ousts the jurisdiction of the courts, as in *Adamolekun* v. *University of Ibadan*.[140] These are general cases on fundamental human rights based on specific provisions. The problem under investigation in this work is that the Constitution has not defined the extent of the derogation from the free exercise of rights and the approach of the Nigerian courts so far has been shapeless. This creates a gap which should be filled to improve societal order.

In the exercise of their powers of judicial review, courts in Nigeria have given decisions on matters of faith that are relevant to the subject matter of this paper. It is pertinent to repeat that in their interpretation the courts have shown an inclination towards American jurisprudence on judicial review of legislative instruments designed to limit the free exercise rights in democratic societies. The case of *Medical and Dental Practitioners' Disciplinary Tribunal* v. *Okonkwo*,[141] deserves special attention here. The issue in this case was the constitutionality of a patient's rejection of a blood transfusion because of his religious beliefs as an adherent to the Jehovah's witness denomination. The Supreme Court held, per Emmanuel Ayoola J.S.C (as he then was) in the lead judgment, that:

> The right to freedom of thought, conscience or religion implies a right not to be prevented, without lawful justification, from choosing one's life, fashioned on what one believes in, and a right not to be prevented, without justification. The sum total of the rights to privacy and of freedom of thought, conscience or religion which an individual should be left alone to choose a course for his life, unless a clear and compelling overriding state interest justifies the contrary. The laws role is to ensure the fullness of liberty when there is no danger to public interest. Ensuring liberty

137 (1971) U.I.L.R. 201.
138 (1982) 2 NCLR 459.
139 (1982) 3 NCLR 166.
140 (1968) NMLR 253.
141 (2001) 19 WRN 1.

> of conscience and freedom of religion is important component of that fullness.[142]

The Supreme Court's attempt to set down a criterion for justifying the state's restriction on freedom of religion is glaring. In this case the Supreme Court of Nigeria held among other things under sections 37 and 38 of the Nigerian Constitution that a patient can refuse medical treatment based on his or her religious belief even to the point of death "… unless a clear and compelling overriding state interest justifies the contrary …" This indicates the apex court's inclination towards the United States of America's strict scrutiny approach without the slightest consideration of Nigeria's state-religion relations and local experience. The Court went further to say that the "… laws role is to ensure the fullness of liberty when there is no danger to public interest." Although the Supreme Court favoured freedom of religion in this case, the problem, however, is what comes within the purview of "a clear and compelling overriding state interest …" especially in a Nigerian environment? What also comes within the purview of "danger to public interest"? This will require the exercise of discretion in the event of conflict between the two competing rights.

In some other cases, the courts' decisions gave more protection to the free exercise rights of the citizens using the American model. These could be seen in the cases of *The Provost, Kwara State College of Education, Ilorin & Ors* v. *Basirat Saliu & Ors*,[143] *Medical & Dental Practitioners Disciplinary Tribunal* v. *Dr. John E.N. Okonkwo*[144] and *Medical & Dental Practitioners Disciplinary Tribunal* v. *Dr. John E.N. Okonkwo*.[145] In the first case, the Court of Appeal held a lower court's denial of the use of the niqab/hijab by a female Muslim student of the College under the pretext of the protection of public safety, public order and protection of the rights of others to be a violation of the free exercise clause in section 38 of the Nigerian Constitution. The Court further held that any such restriction or derogation must be by the Constitution itself or through a law that is reasonably justifiable in a democratic society as envisaged under section 45 (defence, public order, morally, health and protection of the rights of others) and not by mere policy. The Court did not however interpret the meaning of 'reasonably justifiable law in a democratic society." It also did

142 Ibid., p. 25.

143 CA/IL/49/2006 delivered on 18 June 2009.

144 (2001) 7 NWLR (PT.711) 206, pp. 244–245.

145 Ibid.

not state what constitutes defence, public order etc for the purposes of derogation from the right.

In the third set of cases, the Supreme Court further reaffirmed that sections 37 and 38 of the Constitution allow a patient, even on the point of death, to refuse a particular medical treatment on religious grounds. Other cases in this category are *Nkpa* v. *Nkume*,[146] *Agbai* v. *Okagbue*[147] and *Ajao* v. *Ashiru*.[148] In these cases, the courts gave more protection to freedom of association on religious grounds. In some similar cases however the courts gave divergent decisions. In the first instance, the High Court of Lagos State gave a divergent decision in the case of *Asiyat Abdulkareem & ors* v. *Lagos State Government & ors*.[149] In this case, the Court held that the hijab worn by female Muslim students infringes the right of other non-Muslim students who will feel inferior to the Hijab-wearing students. How likely is this? What are the grounds for this decision? The case is currently before the Court of Appeal. In another case, the Court of Appeal distinguished freedom of religion from the right to life in *Esunabor* v. *Faweya*[150] in terms of their importance. The case involved a Jehova witness's (the Appellant) refusal to give consent to a blood transfusion for her child on the ground of her faith. The police carried out the blood transfusion based on an order from a magistrate's court to that effect. After the child was discharged from hospital, the Appellant made efforts to quash the order of the magistrate's court. The High Court refused to discharge the order and the Court of Appeal further affirmed the decision of the magistrate's court. In its judgment, the appellate court condemned the attitude of the Appellant and described it as 'illegal and despicable which must be condemned in the strongest terms".[151]

What reason could account for this departure? In all these cases, the reasonableness tests applied in the decisions are not clear. What is clear from the whole narration is that there is no specific device for testing the reasonableness or otherwise of this type of restrictions in Nigeria. It should be noted that this paper acknowledges the fact that in construing the meaning of justifiability and reasonability of laws in democratic societies for the purpose of doing a constitutional and human rights discourse of laws such as the Islamic Preaching Board Laws, Nigerian courts are entitled to look elsewhere

146 (2001) 6 NWLR (Pt.710) 543.

147 (1991) 7 NWLR (Pt.204) 391.

148 (1973) 8 NSCC 525.

149 Suit No. ID/151M/13 delivered on 17 October 2014 pp. 13 & 14.

150 (2009) All FWLR (Pt.478) 380.

151 Ibid., p. 397.

for guidance. In doing so, Nigerian courts may resort to judicial borrowing to select persuasive authorities from other jurisdictions whether Common Law or not to to deal with the problem.[152]

It should be noted that nearly every legal system today wrestles with this type of problem. Although resemblance to non-Common Law jurisdictions may be slightly more remote with Nigeria, they can still be relevant in providing different outlooks mainly on principles that have universal validity, such as in the area of the principle of freedom of religion. As a universal right, constitutions and laws should be construed in ways that respect this fundamental principle, recognising that although it is universal, it can and should be implemented in different ways in different cultural and historical settings.

The aim here is to list the range of options open to Nigeria in the light of the experience of other nations. The additional task in this paper is to recommend one out of many options that suits the Nigerian environment. In the words of Belgore JSC (as he then was):

> *It is always of great help to know the line of thinking jurisprudentially in other countries' courts with constitutional provisions resembling our own; nonetheless* our Constitution must always remain a creature of its own circumstances and must always be interpreted in its own location and meaning.[153]

Justice Fatai Williams, C.J.N. (as he then was) further held that:

> It is in the end the wording of the Nigerian Constitution itself that is to be interpreted and applied, and this wording can never be overridden by the extraneous principles of other constitutions which are not explicitly incorporated in the formulae that have been chosen as the frame of this Constitution.[154]

152 *Ogugu* v. *State* (1998) 1 HRLRA 167, p. 189.

153 Ibid., p. 211.

154 *Adegbenro* v. *Akintola and Aderemi* (1962), All N.L.R. 454, p. 479 (per Viscount Radcliffe in his judgment for the Privy Council), quoted in *Attorney-General Bendel State* v. *Attorney-General of the Federation* (1981), 10 S.C. 1, 3 NCLR 1, 1981 NSCC, 314 at 331.

Options for Nigeria

Different countries have applied different judicial review mechanisms in striking a balance between the regulatory power of the state and the citizen's right to freedom of religion. In this section, the United States of America, Germany, Canada and the decisions of the European Court of Human Rights will be considered. At the end of the day, one approach will be recommended for application in Nigeria.

The United States of America

In the United States of America, the Establishment Clause in the American Constitution separates state and religion[155] and therefore all interpretation using the three-legged standard is aimed at maintaining this particular state-religion configuration. So far, the American jurisprudence in this regard has only yielded unstable results. In fact, Claudia E. Haupt[156] quoted Thomas B. Colby's description of the American test as "a dizzying array of widely divergent interpretations of the Establishment Clause". The different balancing mechanisms that exist in the United States of America today are the "minimum and strict scrutiny" standards of review for non-establishment clause cases[157] on the one hand and the lemon, endorsement, coercion, denominational, original and the ceremonial tests[158] on the other for conflicts that relate to the establishment clause. Nigeria cannot learn from this confused and unstable system.

---

155 The text of the First Amendment to the American Constitution provides that "Congress shall make no law respecting an establishment of religion or prohibiting the free exercise thereof."

156 Haupt, C.E., *Religion-State Relations in the United States and Germany: The Quest for Neutrality* (Cambridge University Press, UK, 2012), p. 1.

157 See *Cantwell* v. *State of Connecticut*, 310 U.S. 296 (1940), *Everson* v. *Board of Education of Ewing Township*, 330 U.S. 1 (1947), *Sherbert* v. *Verner*, 374 U.S. 398 (1963), *Lemon* v. *Kurtzman*, 403 U.S. 602 (1971), *Wisconsin* v. *Yoder*, 406 U.S. 205 (1972), *United States* v. *Lee*, 455 U.S. 252 (1982), *Employment Division, Department of Human Resources of Oregon* v. *Smith*, 494 U.S. 872 (1990), *Church of Lukumi* v. *Babalu Aye, Inc.* v. *City of Hialea*, 508 U.S. 520 (1993), *Locke* v. *Davey*, 540 U.S. 712 (2004), *Christian Legal Society* v. *Martinez*, 130 S.Ct. 2971 (2010), *Arizona Christian School Tuition Organization* v. *Winn*, 131 S.Ct. 1436 (2011) and *Hosanna-Tabor Evengelical Lutheran Church and School* v. *Equal Employment Opportunity Commission*, 132 U.S. 694 (2012). For a collection of these cases see Vincent, P.M., *Religious Liberty and the American Supreme Court: The Essential Cases and Documents* (Rowman & Littlefield Publishers, Inc, 2013). Only *Sherbert* was not reported in the book.

158 All these tests are thoroughly discussed in the cases cited in note 25 above.

In addition, Nigeria's state-religion relations and local experience are different from those in the United States of America.

Germany

In Germany, there is a stable balancing mechanism which is aimed at "creating practical concordance" between two conflicting constitutional rights.[159] It has greatly influenced decisions of the European Court of Human Rights. The German Basic Law protects the freedom of religion of all people in its territory.[160] But in practice the government gives substantial financial support to the Church in financial matters, religious education issues and other humanitarian services of the Church.[161] In this regime, the discrimination shown in the support given is justified by "objective differences" among religions.[162] In Germany, Roman Catholics are the dominant religious group and on that basis have an agreement with the government called "Concordat" which has the status of a treaty.[163] This makes it different from other minority religious groups. Thus it follows that in the event of conflict between government regulatory power and the citizen's freedom of religion, the balancing mechanism takes the "Concordat" into account for the purpose of resolution. In contrast to Germany, Nigeria does not relate with any particular religious group in the way in which the government in Germany relates to the Roman Catholic Church although it strongly identifies with the religions of Islam and Christianity in its practices at both horizontal and vertical levels. This makes the approach in Germany inappropriate for Nigeria.

Canada

The Canadian standard is based on the wording of section 1 of the Canadian Charter which makes provision for the limitation of the freedom of religion

---

159 See: Reitz, J.C., "Freedom of Religion and Its Limitations: Judicial Standards for Deciding Particular Cases to Maintain the State's Secular Role in Protecting Society's Religious Commitments," in Otten, P., [what is missing here?] et al. (eds), *Comparative Perspectives on Sharia in Nigeria*, Spectrum Books Limited, Ibadan, 2005, p. 229.

160 The Grundgesetz of 1949 provides in Article 4 that: 1- "Freedom of Creed, of conscience, and freedom to profess a religious or non-religious faith are inviolable. 2- The undisturbed practice of religion is guaranteed."

161 Durham, C.W., "Patterns of Religion State Relations," in: Witte, J. Jr. & Green, M.C. (eds), *Religion & Human Rights: An Introduction* (Oxford University Press, New York, 2012), pp. 360–378.

162 Ibid., 367.

163 Ibid.

clause.[164] This standard partly resembles what is obtained at the European Court of Human Rights and in the United States of America. It requires any law that seeks to limit the citizens' enjoyment of these rights to possess some features. These are "sufficiently important objective", "rational connection", "a least drastic means" and "proportional effect." The Canadian test is otherwise known as the "Oakes Test balancing mechanism."[165] The problem with this test is in the determination of the requirements of "sufficiently important objective", "rational connection", "a least drastic means" and "proportional effect". They may be construed in a different way in another country due to differences in state-religion relations and local experience.

The European Court of Human Rights

The application of the principle of 'margin of appreciation' in the approach of the European Court of Human Rights on this matter makes the court's approach more suitable to the Nigerian environment than the other approaches discussed above. Through the application of this doctrine, the court attaches importance to states' local experiences and other peculiarities in their decisions.

Margin of Appreciation

In the context of the European Convention on Human Rights, the "doctrine of margin of appreciation" can be defined as the latitude of respect or error which the European Court of Human Rights will allow to national legislative, executive, administrative, and judicial bodies before it declares the actions of states or their organs valid or invalid 'derogation' from the Convention. The Court clarified the doctrine first in the case of *Handyside* v. UK[166] which borders on restriction placed on freedom of expression. In this case, the Court considered whether a conviction for possessing an obscene article could be justified by virtue of Article 10 (2) of the Convention as a limitation on freedom of expression, which was necessary for the 'protection of morals'. The Court stated:

> ....state authorities are in principle in a better position than the international judge to give an opinion on the exact content of those requirements (of morals) as well as on the 'necessity' of a 'restriction' or 'penalty'

164 The Canadian Charter of Rights and Freedoms provides that "The rights and freedoms set out in the Canadian Charter are subject only to such reasonable limits prescribed by law as can be demonstrably justified in a free and democratic society."

165 See: R *v. Oakes*, 1 SCR 103 (1986).

166 *Handyside* v. *United Kingdom* A 24 (1976); 1 EHRR 737 48–49.**

> intended to meet them … Nevertheless, Article 10 (2) does not give Contracting States an unlimited power of appreciation. The Court … is empowered to give the final ruling on whether a 'restriction' or 'penalty' is reconcilable with freedom of expression as protected by Article 10. The domestic margin of appreciation thus goes hand in hand with European supervision.[167]

In addition to the Court's observation, language difference is a major diversive influence among members of the European Convention. On top of these, each member maintains its own unique Constitution, laws and instrumentalities bearing upon the protection of basic rights. It is in the light of these differences that it becomes necessary for the Court to allow a margin of appreciation.

The Convention provides for a two-stage review of complaints by States Parties, individuals, companies, etc. alleging violations of rights guaranteed in the Convention. The system is dependent on the defendant's state repairing any breach of the norm as determined by the Court. These structural arrangements create a vertical tension between the international and national authorities. This tension is worsened by the conflict between the grant to the Convention organs of supervisory power over the states' obligations and the authority granted to States Parties in several Articles of the Convention to restrict rights. To strike a balance in this conflict, the European Court of Human Rights uses the doctrine of margin of appreciation or discretion among other methods. This is partly because the conception of morals changes from time to time and from place to place: there is no uniform conception of morals.

Furthermore, in the case of *Otto-Preminger-Institut* v. *Austria*[168] it was established that, just as in the case of morals, "it is not possible to discern throughout Europe a uniform conception of the significance of religion in society". "Even within a single country such conceptions may vary."[169] In this case the right of freedom of expression was directed against the religious freedom of others. An association had been prevented from showing a satirical film purporting to be set in heaven due to concerns about offending Roman Catholics. The Court could not establish what constituted a permissible interference with the exercise of the right to freedom of expression if there was a conflict with respect to the religions of others. Therefore a certain margin of appreciation has been left to national authorities in assessing the extent of the necessity of such interference. However, the state's margin of appreciation cannot be a wide one

167 Ibid., at paras 48–49.

168 *Otto-Preminger-Institut* v. *Austria* (1994) 19 EHRR 34.

169 Ibid., para. 50.

as "an interference with the right to freedom of expression may exceptionally be permitted" must be narrowly interpreted.[170]

But scholars have criticised this doctrine, arguing that the idea that in the absence of a uniform conception of public morals in Europe contracting states are better placed to assess local values and their application to particular cases lends weight to the idea of moral relativism and compromising the universality of human rights.[171] Commentators have addressed the problem of the supervisory function, endeavouring to reduce the discretion of the states and to impose a stricter standard of supervision. In *Sunday Times* v. UK,[172] the Court held that the scope of the margin of appreciation is subject to the objectivity of the interest to be protected. The Court drew a contrast between the relative objectivity of two interests which constitute a ground for limitation: one is "maintaining the authority and impartiality of the judiciary". The second one is the '"rotection of morals". The former left a narrower margin to the state, since it was objectively ascertainable, whilst the latter was subject to a wide notion of what "morals" were.[173] As far as the scope of this doctrine is concerned, it is applied differentially, with the degree of discretion allowed to the state varying according to the context.[174] A state is allowed considerable discretion in cases of public emergency.

Furthermore, the application of the doctrine will be broad in a situation where there is no harmony among the Member States that constitute the Council of Europe, on the comparative importance of the interest at stake or as to the best way to protect it, particularly where the matter is on some moral issues. The diversity of particular practices among the states and the lack of agreement among them on especially on some moral or ethical issues is one situation that neccisstates the application of the doctrine in Europe. A good example is the regulation of the wearing of religious symbols in educational institutions and the lack of agreement among member states that has necessitated the application of the doctrine on the wearing of religious symbols in educational institutions in European states.

At the other extreme, the margin of appreciation is restricted where an essential feature of an individual's existence is at stake. The margin of appreciation

170 *Otto-Preminger-Institut* v. *Austria* (1994) 19 EHRR 34, Para. 48.

171 Marshall. J., *Personal Freedom through Human Rights Law?* (Martinus, Nijhoff Publishers 2009), p. 42.

172 *Sunday Times* v. *United Kingdom* A 30 (1979) 2 EHRR 245 PC. [what does this mean?] 27.

173 Ibid., at 28.

174 O'Boyle, H., & Warbrick. [initial], *Law of the Convention of the European Court of Human Rights* 2nd edition, (Oxford University Press, 2011), p. 13.

is reduced almost to vanishing point in certain areas, as where the justification for a restriction is the protection of the authority of the judiciary. In the case of *Leyla Sahin* v. *Turkey*[175] it was shown that the margin of appreciation is narrower for negative obligations of the state arising from the Convention.[176] It has been argued in the case law of the Court that the nature of the aim of the restriction and also the nature of the activities involved will affect the scope of the margin of appreciation. The Court has established, for example, that the margin of appreciation will be narrow when an intimate area of one's sexual life is involved[177] or when it focuses on the inner core of the right to respect one's private life.[178] Yet the margin of appreciation is said to be more extensive where the protection of morals[179] is in issue, as outlined above, and in the realm of religious beliefs where a variety of diverse practices is said to exist.

It is important to note that this doctrine indicates that the overall scheme of the Convention is that the primary responsibility for the protection of human rights is on the Contracting Parties. The Court is there to monitor their actions, exercising a power of review.[180] In terms of the duty of the Court to review national decisions, it was outlined in the abovementioned case of *Handyside* v. *UK*[181] that the Court examines the relevant case, relying on the facts and arguments and evidence adduced by the applicant in the domestic legal system and at the international level. "The Court must decide ... whether the reasons given by the national authorities to justify the actual measures of 'interference' they take are relevant and sufficient ..."[182] The supervision concerns both the aim of the measure challenged and its "necessity", it covers not only the basic legislation but also decisions applying it, even one given by an independent court. The Court's supervision would be illusory if it did no more than examine the decisions delivered by the competent national courts in isolation;, it must view them in the light of the case as a whole. The Court must decide, on the basis of the data available to it, whether the reasons given by the national authorities to justify the actual measures of "interference" they take are relevant and sufficient.[183]

175 *Leyla Sahin* v. *Turkey* 2005-XI; 44 EHRR 99.

176 Ibid.

177 *Dudgeon* v. *United Kingdom* A 45 (1983) 4 EHRR 149 PC.

178 *Odievre* v. *France* 42326/98. 2003.

179 *Müller* v. *Switzerland* A 133 (1988); 13 EHRR 212, para. 35–6 39 [these numbers don't seem to make sense].

180 Harris, O'Boyle, *supra*.

181 *Handyside* v. *United Kingdom* A 24 (1978), 1 EHRR 737.

182 Ibid., at para. 48 PC.

183 Ibid., at paras 49–50.

The question arose in *Sunday Times* v. *UK*[184] whether the review function of the Court was restricted to examining whether the authorities had acted in good faith in assessing what the Convention allowed. It was established that "[g]ood faith, even the good faith of an independent decision-maker like a court, will not be sufficient of itself."[185] The margin of appreciation doctrine serves as a mechanism by which a tight rein is kept on state conduct, depending on the context.[186] The provision also covers "acts which are aspects of the practice of a religion or belief in a generally recognized form". The group of Articles 8–11 contains very similar limitation clauses (2) in each Article. The difference between these limitation clauses lies in the differences between the legitimate aims sought to be protected.

Margin of Appreciation, the European Court of Human Rights and Islamic Preaching Board Laws

The European Court of Human Rights relies generally on the principle of margin of appreciation in assessing whether an obstruction is "proportionate" to a particular "legitimate aim". Under this principle, the Court permits the state to make the initial assessment of whether the intrusion is justified.[187] Over the years, the Court has adopted five criteria based on the wording of the limitation clause in Article 9 of the Convention to interpret the principle as it relates to limitation clauses on freedom of religion. The criteria are as follows:

a. the identification of the right;
b. the identification of the intrusion;
c. consideration of whether the hindrance is prescribed by law;
d. determining what objectives, legitimate aims or interests are sought to be protected by the meddling; and
e. deciding whether the intrusion is necessary in a democratic society; whether the state has given cogent reasons for the interference and those reasons are proportionate to the limitation of the applicant's enjoyment of his right, in which connection the margin of appreciation is the most important.

This presupposes that a restriction may be justified if it is prescribed by law and has a legitimate aim: public safety; the protection of public order, health or

184 *Sunday Times* v. *United Kingdom* A 30 (1979), 2 EHRR 245 246.
185 Ibid.
186 Harris, O'Boyle, *supra*.
187 Ibid., pp. 349–351.

morals; the protection of the rights and freedoms of others; and if it is "necessary" or rather "reasonable" in a democratic society. In religious freedom cases the identified right will be freedom to manifest one's religion or belief. The restriction is the state's action which burdened the citizen's right to manifest his or her religion or belief under the Constitution.

The "Prescribed by Law" Requirement

The "prescribed by law" requirement is that the law must be accessible to the citizen and, second, it must be unambiguous in order to enable the citizen to control his conduct: he must be able to foresee to a degree that is reasonable in the circumstances the consequences which a given action may entail.[188] For domestic law to meet these requirements it must protect against arbitrariness by public authorities. In a democratic society where the rule of law applies government officials are not granted unfettered power to exercise discretion in cases of fundamental human rights. Consequently, the law must define the scope of such discretion and the manner of its exercise. In this regard, the case of *Hasan and Chaush* v. *Bulgaria*[189] is relevant. In that case, the European Court of Human Rights held that the limitation on the internal organisation of the Muslim community and the citizens' freedom of religion was not "prescribed by law" because it was arbitrary and was based on legal provisions which allowed an unfettered discretion to the executive and did not meet the required standards of precision. In *Kuznetsov* v. *Russia*[190] the Court found no legal basis for breaking up a religious event conducted on premises lawfully rented for that purpose, the hindrance was not "prescribed by law". The Court did not even proceed to determine whether the meddling of the state pursued a legitimate aim and was necessary in a democratic society.

There are other relevant cases on religious holidays. In states where a secular calendar operates public holidays and regular days of rest are prescribed. Such secular calendars are normally designed to accommodate the requirements of some religious events or important occasions. Problems may arise where the government appears to show a preference for some religious groups over others. A relevant case in this regard is *Kosteski* v. *Former Yugoslav Republic of Macedonia*.[191] This case concerns the right to observe holidays of one's professed religion, which is rooted in the manifestation of religious freedom. The applicant employee was fined for being absent from work on Muslim holiday.

188 *Sunday Times* v. *United Kingdom* A 30 (1979) 2 EHRR 245, para. 49.
189 *Hasan and Chaush* v. *Bulgaria*, 2000-XI.
190 *Kuznetsov and others* v. *Russia*, 184/02 2007.
191 *Kosteski* v. *Former Yugoslav Republic of Macedonia*, Application No. 55170/00, 2006.

The Court was concerned about the sincerity of the petitioner's belief. The Court had not considered it unreasonable to view absence without permission to be a disciplinary matter, since some level of substantiation must be required to avoid any negative consequence imposed on the employee by the employer. The fine for absence was not disproportionate and might, in the circumstances of this case, be regarded as justified in terms of the twin requirements of "as prescribed by law" and "necessary in a democratic society" for the protection of the rights of others. Accordingly, there had not been any violation of Article 9 of the Convention.

In a recent case, *Gütl* v. *Austria*,[192] the applicants were Jehovah's Witnesses who were not covered by the statutory exemption of the Austrian alternative service law allowing an exemption from military service for ministers of recognised religious societies. The Court observed that the autonomous existence of religious communities is indispensable for pluralism in a democratic society and is, thus, an issue at the very heart of the protection Article 9. However, the applicant had been discriminated against on the ground of his religion as a result of the application of the abovementioned discriminatory provision. There had therefore been a violation of Article 14 taken in conjunction with Article 9 of the Convention.

Legitimate Aims

The need to maintain public order was justified in *Cha'are Shalom Ve Tsedek* v. *France*.[193] The applicant association alleged that the French authorities had refused to grant approval necessary for access to slaughterhouses with a view to performing ritual slaughter in accordance with the ultra-orthodox religious prescriptions of its members. The Court maintained that such interference of the state was prescribed by law and pursued a legitimate aim, namely the protection of public health and public order. There was in the present case a reasonable relationship of proportionality between the means employed and the aim sought to be realised. The margin of appreciation left to the state "particularly with regard to establishment of the delicate relations between the State and religions" had not been too excessive or disproportionate; it was compatible with Article 9(2).

In the case of *Manoussakis and ors.* v. *Greece*[194] there were public order grounds to justify making the setting up of a place of worship subject to approval by the state. The applicants maintained that their conviction by the

192 Available at http://echr.ketse.com/doc/49686.99-en-20050201/view/, accessed 19 January 2018 at 9am.

193 *Cha'are Shalom Ve Tsedek* v. *France*, 27417/95 2000.

194 *Manoussakis and Ors* v. *Greece*; European Court of Human Rights, 59/1995/565/651. 1996.

Heraklion Criminal Court infringed Article 9 of the Convention. The Court was of the opinion that the impugned conviction had such a direct effect on the applicant Jehovah's Witnesses' freedom of religion that it could not be regarded as proportionate to the legitimate aim pursued: the protection of public order, and accordingly there was a violation of Article 9. The Court held that "in delimiting the extent of the margin of appreciation in the present case the Court must have regard to what is at stake, namely the need to secure true religious pluralism, an inherent feature of the notion of a democratic society ..." The Court followed *Manoussakis and ors.* v. *Greece* in *Metropolitain Church of Bessarabia and ors.* v. *Moldova*[195] in recognising that states are "entitled to verify whether a movement or association carries on ostensibly in pursuit of religious aims, activities which are harmful to the population." The Court upheld the state's claim that refusing to recognise the applicant Church was intended to protect public order and safety.

The next legitimate aim is "the protection of the rights and freedoms of others". The European Court of Human Rights recognised improper proselytism as a legitimate ground upon which citizens' free exercise rights can be restricted in order to protect the rights of others in a democratic society. In *Kokkinakis* v. *Greece*[196] Mr. Kokkinakis, a Jehovah's Witness, had been sentenced to imprisonment and had been arrested several times in the past for the offence of proselytism in Greece. The Court had consistently held that:

> a certain margin of appreciation is to be left to the Contracting States in assessing the existence and extent of the necessity of an interference, but this margin is subject to European supervision ... The Court's task is to determine whether the measures taken at national level were justified in principle and proportionate.

In this case, the Court must have weighed the requirements of the protection of the rights and liberties of others against the conduct of the applicant convincing his neighbour to convert to another religion, amounting to proselytism. The Greek courts established the liability of Mr. Kokkinakis; however they failed to specify in what way he had attempted to convince his neighbour by improper means. Accordingly, Mr. Kokkinakis's conviction could not be justified in the circumstances of the case by a pressing social need. "The contested measure therefore does not appear to have been proportionate to the legitimate aim pursued or, consequently, necessary in a democratic society ..." This case was

195 *Metropolitan Church of Bessarabia and ors.* v. *Moldova*, (2002) 35 EHRR 306, para. 111.

196 *Kokkinakis* v. *Greece* (14307/88), 1993.

invoked by the Court in the case of *Larrissis and Ors.* v. *Greece*[197] where the prosecution, conviction and punishment of the applicant for the offence of proselytism amounted to infringement of their right to manifest their religion or belief. The Greek government reasoned that relevant actions were taken against these applicants with the aim of protecting the rights and freedoms of others. The Court argued that the impugned measures essentially pursued the legitimate aim of protecting the rights and freedoms of others, making a reference at this point to the foregoing *Kokkinakis* case. The cases mentioned above demonstrated that proselytism may be important in the context of the legitimate aim of protecting the rights and freedoms of others, and states enjoy a wider margin of appreciation. The term "protecting the rights and freedoms of others" implies the case where religious freedom conflicts with another right in the Convention.

Necessary in a Democratic Society

What does "necessary" mean in this context? In the case of *Handyside* v. *United Kingdom*,[198] the Court explained its meaning as follows:

> The Court notes ... that, whilst the adjective 'necessary', within the meaning of article 10 para. 2, is is not synonymous with 'indispensable' ... neither has it the flexibility of such expressions as 'admissible', 'ordinary', 'useful', 'reasonable' or 'desirable'. Nevertheless, it is for the national authorities to make the initial assessment of the reality of the 'pressing social need' implied by the notion of 'necessity' in this context ...

According to this decision, necessity implies that the obstruction of the right should match up to 'a pressing social need'. It should also be proportionate to the legitimate aim pursued. So, member states tates have a certain margin of appreciation in evaluating whether such a need exists at all. But it is for the Court to decide finally on reconcilability of a particular restriction with the rights protected by the Convention.

Impartiality

In the case of *Hasan and Chaush* v. *Bulgaria*, the Court emphasised that the role of the state was to remain unbiased in its management of religious groups in its sphere of influence. The Court held in conclusion that "a failure by the

---

197 *Larissis and Ors.* v. *Greece* (140/1996/759/958–960) 1998. paras 44, 78; *Otto-Preminger-Institute* v. *Austria* (1994) 19 EHRR 34, paras 46–47.

198 *Handyside* v. *Uk*, 24 Eur.Ct. H.R (ser.A)48 (1976).

authorities to remain neutral in the exercise of their powers … must lead to the conclusion that the state meddled with the believer's freedom to manifest their religion." Unsurprisingly, the same approach has been adopted in cases brought by religious communities themselves. The relevant case here is *Metropolitan Church of Bessarabia* v. *Moldova*, which concerned the refusal of the Moldovan authorities[199] to grant official recognition to the applicant Church, which had the practical effect of making both the Church as an organisation and the religious activities of its adherents unlawful. The Court said that "in exercising its regulatory power in this sphere and in its relations with the various religions, denominations and beliefs, the state has a duty to remain neutral". Such duty to remain impartial has been re-iterated on many occasions and it is clear that any evidence that the state has failed to act in such a fashion in its dealings with religious bodies will require justification under Article 9(2) if it is not to amount to a breach of Article 9.

The state's impartiality is of particular importance for issues concerning religious clothing and religious symbols. The cases considered below established that the state must remain neutral at all times. In some cases, as indicated below, the Court has gone even further and suggested that states are under a variety of positive obligations with regard to the freedom of religion and belief. In the case of *Leyla Sahin* v. *Turkey*, the Court referred to its having "frequently emphasized the state's role as the impartial organizer of the exercise of various religions".

In cases such as *Kokkinakis* v. *Greece* and *Larrisis and Ors.* v. *Greece* it emphasised that the role of the state was to ensure that there was a "level playing field" between believers (and between believers and non-believers). This has put the state in a rather different position from that which it previously occupied. Rather than being required to ensure that it remains neutral and impartial in its dealings with religions and with believers, its role becomes one of ensuring that religious life within the state is neutral and impartial, which is an important difference. Neutrality and impartiality means that the state should be disinterested in the internal affairs of organisation unless such affairs have tendencies that can endanger public order, health, morals and the rights and freedoms of others. In this regard, the state is expected to respect the principle of autonomy as it relates to organisations.

For example, in the case of *Serif* v. *Greece*, the Court said that "in democratic societies the state does not *need* to take measures to ensure that religious

199 *Metropolitan Church of Bessarabia and ors.* v. *Moldova* (2002) 35 EHRR 306, para. 116. 91 [are these numbers correct?]; *Kokkinakis* v. *Greece* (14307/88) 1993. 92 [????] Judgment of 24 February 1998, RJD-1998-1, 23 EHHR 329.

communities are brought under a unified leadership".[200] Such an approach casts the state in the role of a "facilitator" of organisational and individual religious freedom. An alternative model, which seems to be the dominant model now, takes a different approach, emphasising the responsibility of the state to ensure the realisation of all Convention rights, emphasising the need for the freedom of religion and belief to be understood in the broader context of democratic society. In the *Kokkinakis* case the Court said that "the freedom of thought, conscience and religion is one of the foundations of a democratic society.... the pluralism indissociable from a democratic society depends on it." It also said that "in democratic societies ... it may be necessary to place restrictions on this freedom in order to reconcile the interests of the various groups and ensure that everyone's beliefs are respected".

Pluralism and Tolerance

If the state is impartial in its dealings with religious organisations and believers, then that will have the practical effect of fostering a climate of pluralism This raises some issues. Most religious systems advance truth claims which are absolutist in nature. For example, in the case of Serif v. Greece the applicant argued that his freedom of religion had been violated by his being convicted of assuming the functions of the leader of the Muslim community in Rodopi, the leadership of which was in dispute. The Court said that "[a]lthough it recognizes that it is possible that tension is created in situations where a religious or any other community becomes divided, it considers that this is one of the unavoidable consequence of pluralism. The role of the authorities in such circumstances is not to remove the cause of tension by eliminating pluralism, but to ensure that the competing groups tolerate each other". This suggests that the state is not only entitled but may be required to exercise a form of oversight over the internal life of religious communities in the interests of ensuring pluralism and tolerance.

A question arises at this point. The state's stepping in and sorting out of the problem may fail to respect the principle of autonomy and demonstrate the degree of neutrality and impartiality which the state must show in its dealings with the believers. These concern the promotion of pluralism and tolerance and respecting the beliefs and autonomy of others by balancing the interest of the government and the interest of the citizens. In the case of *Metropolitan Church of Bessarabia* v. *Moldova* the Government had argued that recognising the applicant Church as a legal entity would broaden the rift within the

---

200 *Serif* v. *Greece*, no. 38178/97, para. 52, ECHR 1999-IX; 94 *Kokkinakis* v. *Greece* (14307/88) 1993, paras 31 and 33.

Orthodox community. The Court rejected this argument, saying that the "state's duty of neutrality … is incompatible with any power … to assess the legitimacy of religious beliefs, and requires the state to ensure that conflicting groups tolerate each other, even when they originated in the same group". In this case the promotion of pluralism seems to have been given increased weight when one was constructing the content of the obligation to ensure that "conflicting groups tolerate each other".

This might be contrasted with the case of the *Supreme Holy Council of the Muslim Community* v. *Bulgaria*, in which the Court placed more emphasis on the role of the state as the promoter of tolerance. In both the *Metropolitan Church of Bessarabia* case and in the *97 Members of the Gladini Congregation* cases, the Court emphasised that "neutrality" and "impartiality" cannot be used to justify a failure to protect the rights of believers under Article 9.

Conclusion

The conclusion to be drawn from this narration is that the function of the Preaching Board Laws in Kano and Borno States is to examine aspiring Islamic religious preachers concerning their qualifications and to issue preaching licences to those applicants found to be suitably qualified; conversely, the laws also criminalise preaching without a licence or in contravention of the terms of a licence. The Islamic preaching laws of Kano and Borno States are designed to regulate Islamic religious preaching only. This raises the first constitutional challenge. In a constitutional democracy where the rule of law is entrenched the state is expected to be neutral and must operate by laws of general application and not laws that target a specific religion.[201]

A second conclusion can be drawn from the composition of the Islamic religious preaching board laws. The power to appoint members of the Preaching Boards vests generally with the governors of the various states. However, in states where emirate councils exist, the government consults them before such appointments are made. One problem that may be envisaged here is what is called "religious gerrymandering"; a situation where the law is enacted with the aim of burdening specific Islamic religious groups with it. For instance, in the 1970s through to early 1980, the Islamic religious groups called Izala experienced discrimination by the government, in favour of the sufi orders and

201 Reitz, J.C., "Freedom of Religion and Its Limitations: Judicial Standards for Deciding Particular Cases to Maintain the State's Secular Role in Protecting Society's Religious Commitments", in Ostien, P., et al., *Comparative Perspectives on Shari'ah in Nigeria*, p. 180.

so was the case with many minority Islamic religious groups in the North. In Kano and Borno, for example, the composition of the boards favours the established sufi Islamic religious groups against the Izala and Boko Haram.

A third problem could arise because the Government might determine the composition of the boards in a way that targets some specific religious groups that may not be comfortable with the religious ideology of the majority religious groups; discrimination and favouratism may result again on the part of government. The discriminatory practices were possible because of a lack of a proper standard of review in the exercise of discretion by the government to determine the reasonableness or otherwise of the ideas and practices of the minority religious groups. In a nutshell, the composition of the Preaching Board Laws may not allow the laws to pass the "prescribed by law" requirement as interpreted by the European Court of Human Rights.

The fourth problem is in the view of the exercise of discretion. Research demonstrates that the process of the exercise of discretion in different legal orders, whether by courts or government officials, is vulnerable to bias, especially where it involves groups whose religious ideologies disagree with those of the majority.[202] This is because such exercise of discretion gives them too much power which they easily abuse or apply arbitrarily. Second, it allows governments to "legitimately" silence its critics, which kills open debate that ensures better public enlightenment. Third, it prevents the survival of unsurpassed arguments to prevail over government positions. Fourth, it allows few scholars to monopolise discourse on religion; sometimes towards a particular doctrine in a particular religion. These observations underscore the importance of the contribution of this paper.

For Kaduna specifically, the conclusion to be drawn is that sections 3, 4, 5, 6 and 7 of the proposed preaching law allow room for the exercise of uncontrolled discretion by men in authority, contrary to the requirement of laws in democratic legal orders. In addition, the law creates room for discrimination against minority religious groups in the state and negates the principle of religious autonomy claims in a democracy. This can be seen, especially, in the composition of the religious preaching committees where only the JNI and the CAN were recognised in both the old and proposed laws.

Another trend that can be inferred is that state regulation of religious preaching in Nigeria has been characterised by violence and discrimination against minority religious groups, which has led to incessant conflicts for years in the region. Here, the history of the proposed Kaduna State Religious Preaching

202 See Richardson, J.T. (ed.) *Regulating Religion: Case Studies from Around the Globe* (Kluwer Academic/Plenum Publishers, New York, 2004), pp. 1–15.

Bill, 2016, particularly intended to replace the state's Regulation of Religious Preaching (amendment) Edicts No. 1 of 1987 and No. 6 of 1996 as discussed in earlier sections is relevant here. The history of the regulation of religion in Northern Nigeria indicates that the influence of established religious groups in the enactment and composition of the religious preaching committees has led to injustice against minority religious groups in the state. The resort to violence by the Nigerian government as a means of social control in intervening in the clash between the two groups also indicates the absence of democratic culture. It is the same trend that provided the impetus for the 2009 Boko Haram insurgency in Nigeria. Nigeria cannot afford to continue with the current extra-judicial means of resolving conflicts between two constitutional right.

A final conclusion that can be drawn is that the proposed Kaduna State Religious Preaching Law of 2016 gave the local authorities power in the discharge of their functions without defining its scope. The consequence of this was arbitrariness, abuse and violation of the right to freedom of religion of the citizens. It may thus be difficult to secure true religious pluralism, which is an inherent feature of the notion of a democratic society, under the present provisions of the proposed religious preaching law.

Another trend that can be inferred from the above discourse is that, the conduct of state regulation of religious preaching in Nigeria has been characterised by violence and discrimination against minority religious groups which led to incessant conflicts in the region for years. The events in Kano, Borno and Kaduna States are instructive. Government negligence in the three states in the enforcement of the religious preaching board laws and the lopsidedness in the composition of the Islamic religious preaching boards which was in favour of dominant religious groups are two factors that contributed to the chaotic situation in the states. On top of these two factors was the Government's resort to violence in order to control the confusion; an action that indicates the absence of democratic culture. It is the same trend that precipitated the 2009 Boko Haram insurgency in Nigeria which is still continuing with indiscriminate taking of innocent lives. Nigeria cannot afford to continue with the current extra-judicial means of solving conflicts between two constitutional rights. Today, the religious preaching board laws can hardly qualify as reasonable as far as democracy is concerned, having regard to the approach of the European Court of Human Rights.

Another important conclusion that can be drawn from the narration is on the nature of Nigeria's religion-state relationship. Research has shown that Nigeria is a country that identifies with religion in almost everything.[203]

203 Ibid., p. 234.

Nigeria is a home to many religions and so religion is a very sensitive matter that government at all levels identifies with.[204] At the vertical level Islam and Christianity are the two religions that the government accommodates. At the horizontal level, where Christians are in the majority, the government identifies more with Christianity and the same thing applies in states where Muslims are in the majority. It is argued elsewhere that Nigeria's state-religion relation is a crossbreed[205] of positive identification regimes at both the vertical and horizontal levels of government. And this is because of the country's history of entanglement with religions at all levels; Islam and Christianity. At the vertical level, Islam and Christianity are the two preferred religions; preferred sets of religious patterns. At the horizontal level, the states show preference to dominant religions in their domain. In this regard, Islam gets preference where Muslims are the majority in a state and Christianity where Christians are in the majority. In summery, different models of positive identification regimes exist at the horizontal level in Nigeria.[206]

It can be inferred from the above discourse that the Preaching Board Laws in the states under study granted government officials unfettered power to exercise discretion in the discharge of their functions. The laws did not however define the scope of such discretion and the manner of its exercise, the consequence of which was arbitrariness, abuse and violation of the free exercise rights of citizens. It may also be difficult to secure true religious pluralism which is an inherent feature of the notion of a democratic society under the present provisions of the Preaching Board Laws. It is valid therefore to conclude that the Preaching Board Laws of the states under study need to be amended to agree with free exercise norms, and by extension to qualify as reasonable laws in a democratic Nigeria. Finally, to be able to determine their reasonableness, an appropriate balancing mechanism based on Nigeria's state-religion relations is needed.

---

204 Hackett, R.I.J., "Regulating Religious Freedom in Africa in *Sharia, Family. And Democracy: Religious Norms and Family Law in Pluralistic Democratic States*", Emory Int'l.L.Rev. (2011) 25 no. 2, pp. 853–879.

205 See Garba, A.S., "Nigeria's State-Religion Relations and Its Legal Implication to Religious Pluralism and by Extension Freedom of Religion", in Coertzen, P., Green, M.C., and Hansen, L. (eds), *Religious Freedom and Religious Pluralism in Africa: Prospects and Limitations* (SUN MeDIA Stellenbosch, South Africa, 2016), pp. 157–175.

206 Ibid.

Recommendation

This paper recommends a balancing mechanism based on Nigeria's state-religion relations and local experience that may be useful to courts and legislators in handling conflicts between the two competing rights in Nigeria. This balancing mechanism calls for the addition of the principle of substantive due process, state-religion pattern and the local experience of countries to the existing criteria used as standards of review in the resolution of conflicts between the competing constitutional rights. The re-assertive nature of the role of religion in the public domain in Nigeria and the world at large indicates the indispensability of religion in the maintenance of public order and security at the global level.[207] Therefore, in the event of conflict between these competing rights in the modern world today, this balancing mechanism is the most appropriate; one that recognises the current role of religion, the local experience of countries and the need to do justice through the application of the principle of procedural due process.

The changing role of religion in the public domain also underscores the importance of considering the state-religion relations of a country as a factor in resolving the kind of conflict in issue. In addition, such a changing role of religion in the public space, especially from 1970 to date in Nigeria and the world at large, has called into question the capacity of secularism theories to address the present challenges of religious crises. Although, Cole Durham, Jr;[208] a well respected scholar on state-religion relations in the world, has posited that it is doubtful to suggest the existence of a correlation between state identification and religion and religious liberty, this paper maintains that such a correlation exists when each country is taken alone without any obsession with generalisation. He himself confirmed in his work that such correlation exist in some countries.[209]

Under this thesis, the state can protect its existing relationship with religion through a valid law envisaged by its Constitution; this suggests that the actions of a religious group can be subjected to the test to determine its reasonability or otherwise. Conversely, where the practice of a religious group in a country agrees with the country's state-religion pattern, it must be allowed. The United

---

207 See Toft, M.D., et al., *God's Century: Resurgent Religion And Global Politics*, W.W. Norton & Company, New York, 2011, pp. 207–223.

208 Cole Durham Jr. W., "Pattern of Religion State Relations"' in Witte, J., Jr. and Green, M.C., *Religion and Human Rights: An Introduction*, Oxford University Press, New York, 2012, pp. 360–361.

209 Ibid.

States of America and Germany are countries that have used their state-religion relations in the determination of the reasonability or otherwise of both governmental and individual actions as shown in the paper.

Part of the local experience of Nigeria for the past twenty years has been managing crises related to religion. Government restriction of the free exercise rights of some religious groups in favour of dominant religious groups in some states of Northern Nigeria has contributed to the crises. Neither the government nor any of the victims has approached the court for judicial determination of the conflict. Even if they had approached the courts, only God knows what will happen considering the mindset of the judges and the people of Nigeria generally on minority religious groups and their ideologies. Another challenge in Nigeria is whether with the present experience the government will allow members of religious groups to determine the meaning of religion for the government.

References

Table of Cases

Nigerian Cases

Attorney-General of Ogun State v A.G. Federation and Ors (1982) 3 NCLR 166
Attorney-General of Bendel State v A.G. Federation & Ors (1982) 3 NCLR 358
Adamolekun v University of Ibadan (1968) NMLR 253
Lakanmi v Attorney-General of Western Region & Ors (1971) U.I.L.R. 201
Ojiegbe & Ors v Ubani & Ors (1961) All NLR 277
R. T. N. B. C. & Anor v The R.T. A. C.O. & Ors (1992)7 NWLR (PT251)
Shodeinde and Ors v Registered Trustees of Ahmadiyya (1983) NSCC 523
Shugaba Darman v Minister of Internal Affairs and Ors (1982) 2 NCLR 459

United States of America's Cases

Cantwell v. Connecticut [310 U.S. 296,303 (1940)]
Canwell v. Connecticut [310 U.S. 296 (1940)]
Christian Legal Society v. Martinez [130 S. Ct. 2971 (2010)]
Church of Lukumi Babalu Aye, Inc v. City of Hialeah [508 U.S. 520 (1993)]
Employment Division v. Smith [494 U.S. 872 (1990)]
Frazee v. Illinois Department of Unemployment Security [80 U.S. (13 Wall) 679(1871)]
Hosanna-Tabor Evangelical Lutheran Church & School v. Equal Employment Opportunity Commission [132 S. Ct. 694 (2012)]
Locke v. Davey [540 U.S. 712 (2004)]
McCollum v. Board of Education [333 U.S. 203 (1948)]

McGowan v. Maryland [366 U.S. 420 (1961)]
Reynolds v. United State [98 U.S. 145 (1879)]
Sherbert v. Verner [374 U.S. 398 (1963)]
Watson v. Jones [489 U.S. 829, 834 (1989)]
Wisconsin v. Yoda [406 U.S. 205 (1972)]

Other Non-Nigerian Cases

Blake v. Associated Newspapers [(2003) EWHC 1960]
Bruker v. Marcovitz [(2007)3 SCR 607]
Free Church of Scotland v. Overtoun [(1904) AC 515 at 644–5]
Handyside v. United Kingdom
Khaira v. Shergil [(2012) EWCA Civ 983]
Kokkinakis v. Greece [260Eur.Ct. H.R.(ser. A) (1993)]
Singh v Eastern Media Group [2010] EWHC (QB) 1260]

Table of Legislation

Bauchi State Religious Preaching (Suspension) Law, 1987
Bauchi State Religious Preaching Law, 1984
Borno State Islamic Religious Preaching Law, 2010
Kano State Religious Preaching Edict, 1985
Katsina State Regulation Religious Preaching Law, 1991
Kebbi State Religious Preaching Board Law, 2004
Jigawa State Religious Preaching Edict, 1985 [inherited from Kano]
Nassarawa State Regulation of Public Preaching Edict, 1986 [inherited from Plateau state]
Niger State Islamic Religious Preaching Edict, 1979
Niger State Islamic Religious Preaching Edict, 1985
Plateau State Regulation of Public Preaching Edict, 1986
Sokoto State Certain Religious Preaching Edict, 1979/1986
Yobe State Religious Preaching Edict, 1994

Table of Conventions

African Charter on Human and Peoples Rights, 1981
International Covenant of Economic, Social and Cultural Rights, 1966
International Covenant on Civil and Political Rights, 1966
The American Convention on Human Rights, 1969
The European Declaration on Human Rights, 1950
The United Nation Declaration on the Elimination of All Forms of Intolerance and of Discrimination Based on Religion or Belief (Declaration on Religion), 1981
Universal Declaration of Human Rights, 1948

Secondary Sources

Books

Abdullahi, S.U., *On the Search for a Viable Political Culture: Reflections on the Political Thought of Shaikh Abdullahi Dan Fodio,* New Nigerian Newspapers Ltd, Kaduna 1984.

Afolayan, F., "Religion and Politics in Colonial Nigeria: The Life and Career of Sir Walter Miller, 1782–1952," in *Religion in Politics: Secularism and National Integration in Modern Nigeria*, ed. Julius, O. Adekunle (New Jersey Inc: Africa World Press, 2009), 37–66.

Aharon, B., *Constitutional Rights and Their Limitations*, Cambridge University Press, U.K. 2012.

Berkey, J.P., *Popular Preaching and Religious Authority in the Medieval Islamic near East*, University of Washington Press, Seattle, 2001.

Brendan, S., *Why Politics Needs Religion: The Place of Religious Arguments in the Public Sphere*, IVF Academic, Illinois, 2006.

Brian, J.G., and Roger F., *The Price of Freedom Denied*, Cambridge University Press, New York, 2011.

Brian, J. Grim and Roger Finke, *International Religion Index: Government Favouritism, and Social Regulation of Religion* (*Interdisciplinary Journal of Research on Religion*), 2006.

Edward, M. and Jonathan. V., *The Power of Religion In The Public Sphere* (Columbia University Press, New York, 2011).

Gumi, A., with Tsiga, I.A., *Where I Stand*, Spectrum Books Ltd, Ibadan, 1992.

Hana, V.O., *Religious Symbols in Public Functions: A Comparative Analysis of Dutch, English and French Justifications for Limiting the Freedom of Public Officials to Display Religious Symbols*, Intersentia, Cambridge, 2012.

Hare, I., and Weinstein, J., *Extreme Speech and Democracy* (Oxford University Press, Oxford, 2009).

Islam, A.M., *Freedom of Religion in Sharia: A Comparative Analysis* (A.S. Noordeen, Kuala Lumpur, 2008.

John, W. Jr., and Christian, M.G., *Religion and Human Rights: An Introduction*, Oxford University Press, New York, 2012.

Loimeier, R., *Islamic reform and political change in northern Nigeria*, North Western University Press, Evanston 1997.

Kuka, M.H., *Religion, Power and Politics in Northern Nigeria*, Ibadan: Spectrum Books Limited, 2011.

Mohammed, B., *Infaq al-Mansur*, ed. C.E.J. Whiting (London, 1957).

Ostien, P., A Survey of the Muslims of Nigeria's *North Central Geo-Political Zone, in: Nigeria Research Network* (*NRN*), *Oxford Department of International Development*, Queen Elizabeth House, Oxford Univerisy (*NRN*) Working Paper No. 1.

Paden, J.N., *Faith and politics in Nigeria: Nigeria as a pivotal state in the Muslim world*, United States Institute of Peace Press, Washington, D.C., 2008.

Paden, J.N., *Muslim Civic Cultures and Conflict Resolution: The Challenge of Democratic Federalism in Nigeria*, Brookings Institution Press, Washington, D.C., 2005.

Peltze, Audrey, *A Survey of Constitutional Challenges to Municipal Regulation of Religious Solicitation and a Suggested Legislative Compromise, Fordham Urban Law Journal*, Volume 11, Issue 4, Article 19, 1982.

Ricardo, R.L., *Islamic Law and Politics In Northern Nigeria*, Africa World Press, New Jersey, 2011.

Saeed, A.G., *The British Policy Towards the Mahdiyya in Northern Nigeria: A Study of the Arrest, Detention and Deportation of Shaykh Said b. Hayat, 1923–1959, Kano Studies*, II/3, 1982–5, 1985.

Salter, M., and Mason, J., *Writing Law Dissertations: An Introduction and Guide to the Conduct of Legal Research*, Pearson Education Ltd, England, 2007.

Shedrack, G.B., (ed) *Religion and PostConflict Peacebuilding in Northern Nigeria* (John Archers Ltd, Ibadan, 2011).

Smith, J.M., 'Redefining Normative Legal Science: Towards an Argumentative Discipline' in: A.P.M. Coomans and F. Grunfeld (eds), *Methods of human rights research*, Intersentia, Antwerp, 2009.

Stephen, V.M., and Christopher, J.S., *Church and State in Five Democracies: The Challenge of Pluralism 2nd* edition (Rowman and Littlefield Publishers Inc, New York, 2009).

Sulaiman, I., *The Islamic State and the Challenge of History: Ideals, Policies and Operation of the Sokoto Caliphate, Mansell, London, 1987.*

Toft, M.D., Philpott, D. and Shah, T.S., *God's Century*, W.W. Norton & Company, London, 2011.

Tomlinson, G.J.F., and Lethem, G.J., *History of Islamic political propaganda in Nigeria*, Waterlow, London, 1927.

Ubah, C.N., *British Measures against Mahdism at Dumbulwa in Northern Nigeria 1923: A Case of Colonial Overreaction, Islamic Culture* I/3, 1976 pages 169–83.

Udoma, U., *History and the Law of the Constitution of Nigeria*, Malthouse Press Ltd, UK, 1994.

Umar, M.S., *Islam and Colonialism: Intellectual Responses of Muslims of Northern Nigeria to British Colonial Rule*, Brill, Leiden & Boston, 2006.

Usman, B.Y., *The Manipulation of Religion in Nigeria 1977–1987*, Vanguard Printers and Publishers, Kaduna, 1987.

Vincent, P.M., *Religious Liberty and the American Supreme Court: The Essential Cases and* Documents (Rowman & Littlefield Publishers, Inc, 2013).

Zahradeen, Nasir B., *The Maitatsine Saga*, Hudahuda Publishing Co., Zaria, 1988.

Edited Books

Adekunle, J.O., (ed) *Religion in Politics: Secularism and National Integration in Modern Nigeria, Africa* World Press, Trenton, NJ 2009.

Allen, D.H., (ed) *The Future of Religious Freedom: Global Challenges*, Oxford University Press 2013.

Barkindo, B.M., "Growing Islamism in Kano City since 1970: Causes, Form and Implications" in: Brenner, L. (ed) *Muslim Identity and Social Change in Sub-Saharan Africa*, Indiana University Press, Bloomington and Indianapolis, 1993 pages 91–105.

Chris, S., Dennis. R.H., and Pauletta, O., (ed) *The Routledge Handbook of Religion and Security*, Routledge, New York, 2013.

Clarke, P., "The Maitatsine Movement in Northern Nigeria in Historical and Current Perspective", in: R.I.J. Hackett, (ed) *New Religious Movements in Nigeria*, E. Mellen Press, Lewiston, N.Y., 1987.

Cristiana, C., Durham, W.C., Jr., and Donlu, T., (eds) *Law, Religion, and Constitution: Freedom of Religion, Equal Treatment, and the Law*, Ashgate Publishing Company, *USA*, 2013.

Gamaliel, J.D., "An analysis of Religion under the 1999 Constitution and Prospects for Peace building in Nigeria" in: Best, G.S., (ed) *Religion and Post Conflict Peace Building in Northern Nigeria* (John Archers, Ibadan, 2011) page 114–115.

Gunn, J.T, in: Witte, J. Jr. & Green, M.C., (eds), *Religion & Human rights: An Introduction*, Oxford University Press, New York, 2012.

Gwandu, A.A., "Aspects of the Administration of Justice In The Sokoto Caliphate And Shaykh Abdullahi Ibn Fodio's Contribution to it", in: Rashid, K.S (ed) *Islamic Law in Nigeria* (Islamic Publications Bureau, Kaduna, 1986) Page 10–27.

Hellel, F., Husain, H., Eric Brown, and Hassan, M., (ed) *Current Trends in Islamists Ideology*, vol. 14, Hudson Institute, New York, 2013.

Hellel, F., Husain, H., Eric Brown, and Hassan, M., (ed) *Current Trends in Islamists Ideology*, vol. 15, Hudson Institute, New York, 2013.

Hellel, F., Husain, H., Eric Brown, and Hassan, M., (ed) *Current Trends in Islamists Ideology*, vol. 16, Hudson Institute, New York, 2014.

Hellel, F., Husain, H., Eric Brown, and Hassan, M., (ed) *Current Trends in Islamists Ideology*, vol. 17, Hudson Institute, New York, 2014.

James, T.R., (ed) *Regulating Religion: Case Studies from Around the Globe*, (Kluwer Academic/Plenum Publishers, New York, 2004).

James, T.R., "Major Controversies involving New Religious Movements", in: Olav Hammer and Mikael Rothstein (eds), *The Cambridge Companion to New Religious Movements* (Cambridge University Press, *UK*, 2012).

John, L., John. K., and Wilfried. S., *Rutledge Handbook of Regionalism and Federalism*, Rutledge, New York, 2013.

Julius, O.A., (ed) *Religion In Politics: Secularism and National Integration in Modern Nigeria*, Africa World Press Inc, New Jersey, 2009.

Kabir, A., "Nature of Legal Research for New Researchers", in: Ahmed, A.B, *Issues in Research Methodology in Law* (ed), Faculty of Law, B.U.K., Kano, 2010.

Kumo, S., "Shari'ia Under Colonialism-Northern Nigeria" in: Alkali, N., et al. (ed) *Islam in West Africa*, Spectrum Books Ltd, Kaduna, 1993 Page 1–22.

Last, M., Reform in West Africa: *The Jihad Movements of the Nineteenth Century*, In: J.F.A. Ajayi (ed), *History of West Africa*, vol. 2, 1987 page 1–47.

Lovejoy, P.E. and J.S. Hogendorn, "Revolutionary Mahdism and Resistance to Colonial Rule in the Sokoto Caliphate, 1905–6" in: *The Journal of African History*, 31/2, (1990) pages 217–244.

Mark, T., Thomas, F., and Cheryl, S., (eds), *Rutledge Handbook of Constitutional Law*, Rutledge, New York, 2013.

Mazrui, A.A., "African Islam and Comprehensive Religion :Between Revivalism and Expansion" in Alkali, N. et al., *Islam in Africa*, Spectrum Books Limited, Ibadan, 1993 Page 247–265.

McConville, M. & Chui, W.H., (eds), *Research Methods for Law*, Edinburgh University Press Ltd, Edinburgh, 2007.

Moreno, P., (ed), *Handbook on Religious Liberty around the World*, Rutherford Institute, Charlottesville, Virginia, 1996.

Pieter, C., Green, M.C., and Len, H., (eds), *Law and Religion in Africa: The Quest for Common good in pluralistic societies*, Sun Media, Stellenbosch, 2015.

Smith, J.M., 'Redefining Normative Legal Science: Towards an Argumentative Discipline' in: A.P.M. Coomans and F. Grunfeld (eds), *Methods of Human Rights Research*, Intersentia, Antwerp, 2009.

Stephen, M.F., (ed) *Law and Religion: A Critical Anthology*, New York University Press, New York, 2000.

Umar, M.S., "Changing Islamic Identity in Nigeria from the 1960s to the 1980s: From Sufism to anti Sufism", in: Brenner, L. (ed.), *Muslim Identity and Social Change in Sub-Saharan Africa*, 154–178, Indiana University Press, Bloomington and Indianapolis, 1993.

Translated Books

Dan Fodio, A., (here: b. Foduye, A.) *Diya al-Umara: A Guide for Rulers Concerning their Demands and Obligations.* With Arabic and English texts, edited and translated by Hamidu Alkali (Centre for Islamic Studies, Usmanu Danfodiyo University, Sokoto, 2004).

Dan Fodio, A., Diya al-Hukkam. Published in Arabic by Dar al-Arabia Li Diba'ati wa al-Nashur (Cairo, n.d.), Hausa Translation Published by Gaskiya Corporation (n.d.) and reprinted by (Sidi Umaru Press, Sokoto, 1984).

Dan Fodio, U., *Kitab al-Farq*, published in Arabic with English translation by M. Hiskett in Bulletin of the School of Oriental and African Studies, 23, (1960).

Gumi, A.M., *Al-aqidah al-sahihah bi muwafiqah al-shari'ah* (*The right belief is based on the shari'ah*), in Arabic with English translation by Dr. M.O.A. Abdul. Ankara: Hilal Publishing House, n.d. [The Arabic text of the Al-aqidah al-sahihah was published in 1972; date of publication of the text with English translation is not given.]

Maghili, M., Bayreuth: *Imprimerie Catholique., The Obligations of Princes: An Essay on Moslem kingship*. Translated from the Arabic by T.H. Baldwin (1932).

Maghili, M., *Sharīʿa in Songhay: The replies of al-Maghīlī to the questions of Askia al-Ḥājj Muḥammad*. Edited and translated with an introduction and commentary by John O. Hunwick. Published for the British Academy by Oxford University Press, London; New York, 1985.

Journal Articles

Christelow, A., "Religious Protest and Dissent in Northern Nigeria from Mahdism to Quranic integralism", *Journal of the Institute of Muslim Minority Affairs*, 6/2, (1985) Pages 375–393.

Clarke, P., "Islamic Reform in Contemporary Nigeria: Aims and Methods", In: *Third World Quarterly* 10/2, (1988), Page 519–538.

Gambo, Y.L., and Omirin, M.M., "Ethno Religious Conflict and Settlement Pattern in Northern Nigeria", *Mediterranean Journal of Social Sciences*, vol. 3 (3), September 2012.

Hackett, R.I.J., "Regulating Religious Freedom in Africa", in: *Sharia, Family, And Democracy: Religious Norms and Family Law in Pluralistic Democratic States*, Emory Int' L.L.Rev., Emory University School of Law Atlanta, Georgia, 2011.

Hiskett, M., "The Maitatsine Riots in Kano, 1980: An Assessment", *Journal of Religion in Africa*, xvii/3 (1987), 209–23.

Lasson, Kenneth, *Incitement in the Mosques: Testing the Limits of Free Speech and Religious Liberty*, 27 Whittier L. Rev. 3, 2005–2006.

Rev. Vishigh, R.I., "The Separation of Church and State: Nigeria's Constitutional Contrivance. Another View", *Current Jos Law Journal* (1998) CJLJ, Vol. 4, No. 4. Pages 107–123.

Reynolds, J., "Good and Bad Muslims: Islam and Indirect Rule in Northern Nigeria". *The International Journal of African Historical Studies*, 34/3, (2001).

Shikyl, S.S., *Judicial Attitude to Human Rights in Nigeria Under Civilian Dispensation*, Vol.3, 1997, Unijos LSJ, Pp. 90–100.

Terwase Sampson, Isaac, *Religious Violence in Nigeria: Causal Diagnosis and Strategic Recommendations to the State and Religious Communities*, African Journal on Conflict Resolution, 2012.

Voll, J.O., "The British, the Ulama, and Popular Islam in the Early Anglo-Egyptian Sudan". *International Journal of Middle East Studies*, 2/3, (1971).

Yadudu, A.H., *The Separation of Church and State: Nigeria's Constitutional Contrivance.* Lawyers Bi-Annual, *Journal of the Nigerian and Comparative Law* (1994), vol. 1&2.

Newspapers

Francis, U., "Nigeria: Boko Haram- Islamic Leaders to vet Clerics." In: Daily Trust Newspaper, page 11, 4 August, 2009.

New Nigerian Newspaper, Paid advertorial by "Katsina State Government." September, 2011.

This Day Newspaper, Nigeria: Borno Approves 150 Preachers for Ramadan," August, 2009.

Unpublished Dessertations

PhD

Anwar, A., *Gardawa, Ulama and the State in Northern Nigeria: the Maitatsine Phenomenon, 1962–1985*. Ph.D. dissertation (unpublished) University of Maiduguri, (1997).

Bako, S., *The Maitatsine revolts: A Socio-Political Explanation of the Islamic Insurrections in Northern Nigeria, 1980–1985*. Ph.D. dissertation (unpublished), Ahmadu Bello University, Zaria. (1992).

Chamberlin, J.W., *The Development of Islamic Education in Kano City, Nigeria, With Emphasis on Legal Education in the* 19th *and* 20th *Centuries*, Ph.D Dissertation (unpublished) Columbia University, (1975).

Wakili, H., *The Phenomenon of Revolts and Riots in Kano, 1983–1995: an historical perspective*. Ph.D. dissertation (unpublished), Bayero University Kano, (1997).

M.A.

Imam, G.A., Malam Lawal Kalarwi: Nazarin Sassan Adabi A Cikin Ayyukansa., M.A. Hausa thesis (unpublished), Department of Hausa, Bayero University Kano, (2005)

Reports

Nigerian Reports

Borno State of Nigeria, *Report of the Commission of Inquiry into the Religious Disturbances in Bullum Kuttu Area of Maiduguri Between the 26th–29th October*, 1982–1983.

Centre for Democratic Research and Training, *Report of a Commissioned Study on the* Ulama *in Contemporary Northern States of Nigeria, Submitted to the Federal Government of Nigeria*. Kano: Mambayya House, Bayero University Kano. (2005).

Da'wah Coordination Council of Nigeria, *The* "Boko Haram" *Tragedy: Responses to 26 of the most commonly asked questions regarding the "Boko Haram" crisis and tragedy* (Da'wah Coordination Council of Nigeria, Minna, Nigeria, 2009).

Federal Government of Nigeria, *Report of Tribunal of Inquiry on Kano Disturbances.* (Federal Government Press, Lagos, 1981).

Federal Republic of Nigeria, *Report of the Jimeta Disturbances Tribunal of Inquiry*, 1984.

Federal Republic of Nigeria, *Views of the Government of the Federation on the Report of the Kano Disturbances Tribunal of Inquiry* (National Assembly Press, Lagos, 1981).

Pew Forum on Religion & Public Life, *Global Restrictions on Religion* (Pew Research Center, Washington, D.C., 2009).

Non-Nigerian Reports

United States Commission on International Religious Freedom's Reports for 2014, 2013, 2012, 2011 and 2010 available at www.uscirf.gov/sites/default/files/USCIRF%20A accessed on the 19th day of October 2015 at 2:00pm.

Memorandum

Middleton, H.H., Memo to Residents, Kano, Zaria, Sokoto and Niger., Missionary Activities in Muslim Centres, 13 December 1926.

www.ingramcontent.com/pod-product-compliance
Lightning Source LLC
Chambersburg PA
CBHW031332230926
51848CB00001B/196